FOR BREW FREAKS, BEAN GEEKS AND THE SIMPLY CURIOUS

THE NORTH
AND NORTH WALES
INDEPENDENT
COFFEE
GUIDE

the INSIDER'S GUIDE TO SPECIALITY
COFFEE VENUES AND ROASTERS

★★★★★★★★★★★

Nº4

Copyright © Salt Media Ltd
Published by Salt Media Ltd 2018
Tel: 01271 859299
Email: ideas@saltmedia.co.uk
www.saltmedia.co.uk

The right of Salt Media to be identified as the author of this work
has been asserted by it in accordance with the Copyright, Designs
and Patents Act 1988.

A catalogue record of the book is available from the British Library.

Salt Media *Independent Coffee Guide* team:
Richard Bailey, Nick Cooper, Sophie Ellis, Kate Fenton,
Ruth King, Kathryn Lewis, Abi Manning, Amy Pay,
Tamsin Powell, Jo Rees, Rosanna Rothery,
Emma Scott-Goldstone, Christopher Sheppard,
Dale Stiling, Mark Tibbles and Selena Young.

Design and illustration: Salt Media

**A big thank you to the *Independent Coffee Guide*
committee** (meet them on page 212) for their expertise
and enthusiasm, **our headline sponsors** Cimbali,
KeepCup and Olam Specialty Coffee, **and sponsors**
Atkinsons Coffee Roasters, Blue Diamond, Cakesmiths,
Shibui Tea and Stephensons Dairy.

Coffee shops, cafes and roasters are invited to be
included in the guide based on meeting strict criteria
set by the committee, which includes use of speciality
beans, being independently run and providing a high
quality coffee experience for visitors.

For information on the Ireland, Scottish, and South West
and South Wales *Independent Coffee Guides*, visit:

www.indycoffee.guide

🐦 @indycoffeeguide

📷 @indycoffeeguide

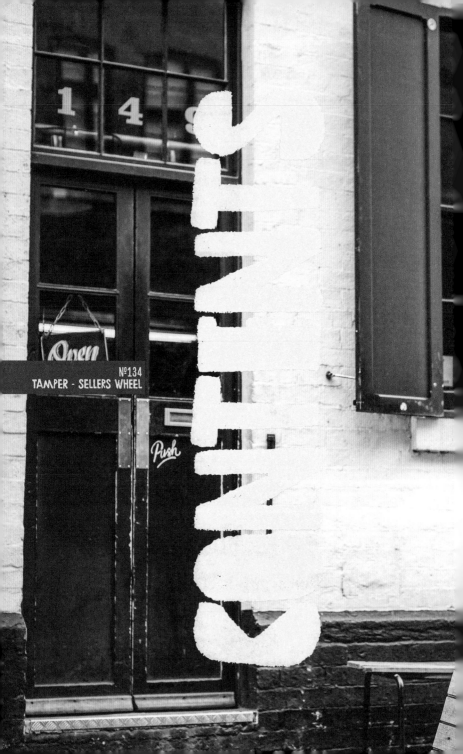

Over the past four years, the pursuit of the perfect cup has taken me to the remotest parts of the UK, and quashed some of my misconceptions about what turns out to be an impeccably caffeinated isle – if you look in the right places.

I can't swear that the intoxicating buzz of silky espresso didn't make Sunderland's coastline even clearer, or that the sugary rush from handmade doughnuts didn't make cruising North Wales' winding lanes even sweeter, but all I know is that I probably wouldn't have wandered quite so far off the beaten track if I wasn't on a quest for quality coffee.

That's the beautiful thing about the ever-expanding speciality community: it not only introduces folk to exceptional brews, it also encourages them to explore new places (while meeting fellow coffee fiends) along the way.

The *Indy Coffee Guide* Instagram has been inundated with pics from your coffee-shop-hopping holidays and roastery road trips this year (shout out to Eliot Dales who visited every venue in the last guide). I hope this bumper edition inspires even more espresso excursions – just remember to send us a postcard.

Here's to caffeinated adventures.

Kathryn Lewis

Editor
Indy Coffee Guides

🐦 @indycoffeeguide
📷 @indycoffeeguide

10 WAYS

TO BE A MORE ETHICAL COFFEE DRINKER

Keen to curb throwaway culture and be kinder to the planet without kicking your speciality habit? Squeeze a few of these simple swaps into your daily routine and your conscience will be as clear as that fruity filter

1 DIG THE DOGGY BAG

WOOF!

If you're defeated by the epic slice of cake accompanying your coffee, don't forget to ask for a doggy bag (bonus points if you take along your own container). Not only will you be super chuffed when round two rolls around later on, but you'll also be saving money and reducing food waste #doublewin.

2 HOME GROWN BEANS

While your chances of stumbling upon coffee plants cultivated down the road are pretty slim, most home brewers are likely to find a local roaster bronzing speciality-standard beans nearby. Head to the back of the guide and you'll discover a treasure trove of North and North Wales roasters – fewer miles to your front door means less CO_2.

CUP-LE UP 3

If your mobile caffeine kicks still come in a plastic-lined paper cup, it's time to ditch the disposable for a reusable model. Every minute, over a million cups make their way to landfill and takeaway coffee plays a big part in the spiralling pile-up.

Speciality coffee shops were championing the reuse revolution before the chains jumped on the bandwagon and most offer a tidy discount if you rock up with a KeepCup. An increasing number of cafes such as Baltzersen's in Harrogate are taking it a step further by banning single-use cups altogether and taking a hit on profits in order to curb throwaway culture.

As the region's penchant for speciality peaks, so do the piles of used coffee grounds heading for the bin. The old grounds are no longer good for brewing coffee, but plants and flowers can't get enough of the stuff, hence the growing number of gardeners taking the soil enhancer off baristas' hands.

And it's not just green-fingered coffee fiends putting the grounds to good use: savvy coffee shops are using them to make products such as soap and face wash.

4 NEW LIFE IN OLD GROUNDS

5 SHOP LOCAL

Speciality coffee shops are often a great place to bag local foodie products and artisan goodies. If you can't pick up provincial preserves, freshly baked loaves or handcrafted chocolate at your fave spot, you should be able to stock up on speciality grade beans.

6 RETRO DAIRY

Remember when milk would appear on your doorstep each morning as if by magic? The milkman is making a comeback and an increasing number of indie dairies are bringing back the daily delivery. Find your local milk float online or ask your nearest coffee shop who's supplying the white stuff. Glass bottles reduce plastic waste and buying from a smaller supplier supports local business.

7 PICK THE LONG(LIFE) STRAW

Yes, you know to swerve plastic straws in favour of a recyclable alternative. Yes, you know a reusable metal one is even better. We'll stop preaching to the converted.

RETURN OF THE TUPPERWARE

8

Picking up grub to-go from your fave cafe? While a lot of speciality shops offer biodegradable packaging, these green disposables have to be disposed of in an industrial composting facility to reap the full benefits (read: not in your average bin). So don't be shy about asking the cafe team to pop lunch in your Tupperware.

9 KICK YOUR LOCAL HANGOUT INTO ACTION

Ask the team at your fave cafe whether they're recycling, taking steps to reduce food waste, sourcing local produce and coffee, and making an effort to become greener. If they're not, ask why. Your questions could be the catalyst for change.

10

SNIFF OUT SUSTAINABLE ROASTERIES

It's not just coffee shops that are working to become more sustainable; roasteries across the region are also taking steps to reduce their carbon footprint. Leeds' North Star has launched a range of retail beans packaged in 50 per cent recycled coffee cups, while Grindsmith's new roastery is bronzing beans on an eco-friendly Loring Smart Roast.

We're for the everyday changemakers

Be part of the change

REGIONS ON THE RISE

FIND YOURSELF REPEATEDLY PLAYING IT SAFE WITH THE ETHIOPIAN SINGLE ORIGIN OPTION? GET READY FOR FRESH FLAVOUR NOTES THANKS TO A NEW BATCH OF UP-AND-COMING COFFEE GROWING REGIONS. WE ASKED THE NORTH'S TRAILBLAZING BEAN HUNTERS FOR THEIR ONES TO WATCH

BURUNDI

HOLLY KRAGIOPOULOS
NORTH STAR COFFEE ROASTERS

WHY BURUNDI?

Its altitude, regular rainfall and abundance of bourbon (a coffee plant varietal) is resulting in the cultivation of exceedingly high-quality coffee.

Ongoing political unrest in the country means that the industry has fallen behind that of its east African neighbours. Yet when I visited last year as a member of the international jury at the Cup of Excellence competition I was blown away by the cup profiles.

The coffee displays incredible character with acidity that can often be sparkling and berry-like, and its versatility makes it suitable for a range of brewing methods.

As the fifth poorest nation in the world, Burundi's coffee-growing potential is a huge opportunity for smallholder farmers to transform their social and economic development. Coffee is the country's largest export, and if we can get responsibly minded speciality buyers on board we could see tangible changes taking place. I feel a personal **responsibility to spread the word about this beautiful place.**

YOU TOOK A RECENT TRIP ...

It was amazing to see an industry in such early stages as the possibilities are so exciting. I met lots of inspirational people – from representatives of the government's agricultural department to smallholder farmers (at washing stations in Kayanza and Ngozi) to dry mill workers.

It was shocking to see how little the smallholder farmers were earning from their crop – $50 USD per year isn't representative of the quality of the coffee and needs to change.

ANY OTHER UP-AND-COMING REGIONS TO LOOK OUT FOR?

The Congo is really coming on as a quality coffee producer; we're seeing improved cleanliness and cup clarity each year.

Brazil is also seeing a rise in speciality grade coffee, with cup profiles more reminiscent of experimental lots from **Costa Rica.**

CHINA
STEPHEN PAWELECK
DJANGO COFFEE CO.

WHY CHINA?

China may be synonymous with tea production, but it's proving to be one of the most up-and-coming origins in the speciality trade.

IT'S A HUGE COUNTRY. WHERE SHOULD WE START?

Coffee predominantly grows in three regions of China: Fujian, Hainan and Yunnan. The first two mainly grow robusta, but Yunnan in the south-west of the country is the trailblazer, concentrating on arabica and the speciality market.

Farmers are realising it's not very sustainable to produce commodity grade coffee and that speciality is more profitable. It's a slow process as farmers need to rethink their approach and processing methods in order to improve quality. Varietals such as typica, bourbon, pacamara and geisha are being planted but will take a few years to mature.

SO IT'S STILL EARLY DAYS?

There's almost no government support in place to help with funding new infrastructure, education and improvement of practices, meaning limited production capacity, competition and quality.

However, our experience with roasting coffee from Yunnan has been really positive. We were lucky enough to meet Christian Steenberg from Indochina Coffee last year and, after a chat about the emergence of coffee in this region, we offered it to our customers. The Fuyan was super clean with flavour notes of golden raisin, plum, toffee, pear and grape.

WELL WORTH SUPPORTING THEN?

Definitely. This particular cooperative is genuinely dedicated to improving its coffee quality, spurred on by a handful of farmers who have long seen the potential of well-processed and carefully selected cherries.

They're now regularly breaking through the 84/85 point mark and, with some of the innovations we've seen on the ground, it's only going to get better.

Photo: Bryon Lippincott for Yunnan Coffee Traders

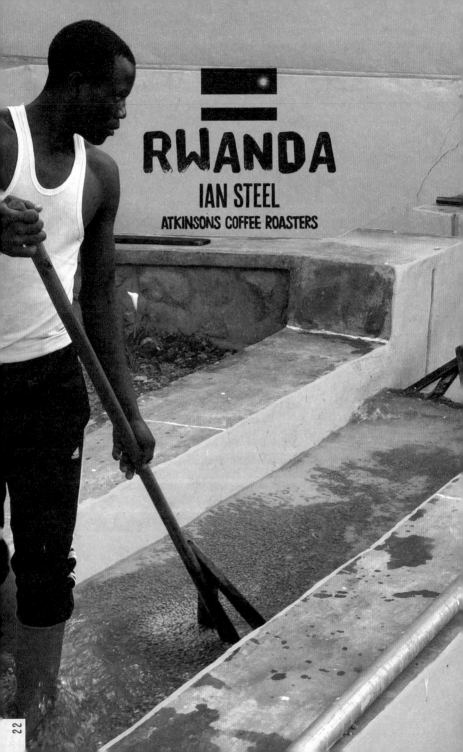

RWANDA

IAN STEEL

ATKINSONS COFFEE ROASTERS

WHY RWANDA?

It has thousands of years of farming heritage: they seem to be able to grow anything instinctively. There was a hiatus in coffee growing during the tragic events of the 90s, but

they've steadily built back up and are now a world repository for 100 per cent bourbon, although we're discovering new cultivars appearing such as jackson.

YOU VISITED RECENTLY?

I was there in June 2018 at the end of the rainy season and the countryside was at its most beautiful. It's so close to the centre of the continent that the elevation starts at 1,600m above sea level, with great coffee grown from there all the way up to 2,500m.

WHAT INSPIRED YOU?

What's exciting about any trip to origin is that it's never just about coffee. It's a privileged glimpse into the sociology, ecology, meteorology and agronomy surrounding people's daily lives. We spent time with A New Beginning, a charity supporting widows and children displaced after the genocide. We visited their school, health centre and new washing station; Kinini Coffee was founded in 2012, giving many farmers the opportunity to grow their first cash crop.

WHAT'S INTERESTING ABOUT RWANDAN COFFEE?

It beautifully hits the sweet spot with soft fruit notes and low acidity. It's not as bright and citrusy as other east Africans; it's more subtle and clean, appealing to those just starting out on their coffee journey.

WHICH OTHER REGIONS DO YOU THINK ARE ON THE RISE?

Myanmar. We contributed to a Kickstarter campaign there and tried some of the first coffee produced which was really exciting. It's another chance for a conflict zone to improve through trade not aid.

Southern India is obviously known for its coffee, but look out for new, quality-over-quantity growers from the Araku Valley in the eastern Ghats.

PGS (Perfect Grinding System)
integrated management system.

*For the highest quality coffee
and the greatest possible flexibility.*

Customisable 4.3"
touch screen display.

*To create a set of custom
settings every time.*

Compact design and hopper
with smart shape.

*To improve visibility from the counter
and simplify refill and cleaning.*

Work cycle integrated
with Inverter motor.

*To ensure low consumption
and constant performance.*

New LaCimbali Elective

PERFECT COFFEE
STARTS THIS WAY.

The quality of a coffee is never just about the bean.
It's never just about the roasting process, and neither is it ever just about that first sip.

FRESHER'S GUIDE TO TASTING COFFEE

WANT TO SWOT UP BEFORE YOUR FIRST CUPPING SESH? NOT SURE HOW TO NAVIGATE TASTING NOTES? WE ASKED PAUL MEIKLE-JANNEY, COFFEE GURU AND CO-FOUNDER OF DARK WOODS COFFEE NEAR HUDDERSFIELD, FOR THE COFFEE TASTING BASICS

ADVENTURES IN FLAVOUR

Coffee of varying quality is consumed around the world for its quick caffeine hit, but a growing band of people have turned to the speciality stuff. And it's in this coffee community that the spectrum of flavours extracted from carefully farmed, processed and roasted beans is being explored.

TASTE IT HOW YOU TAKE IT

In the same way that everyone has a preference when it comes to taste, most coffee drinkers have a favoured brew style. So whether you enjoy espresso, drip filter or batch brew, the best way to taste coffee (as a consumer) is to drink it how you'd serve it.

Tasting coffee is essentially about the balance of three main flavour profiles. As you sip, think about the following:

ACIDITY

This refers to organic acids such as citric in lemons or malic in apples. What kind of acidity is in the coffee?

SWEETNESS

How sweet is the coffee? Is it a sugary sweetness or something more complex?

BITTERNESS

How bitter is the coffee? Does it work with the acidity and sweetness?

These three factors will depend on where in the world the beans were grown, the bean variety (robusta or arabica and their various cultivars), the way in which they were processed (honey, natural or washed) and the roast (light, medium or dark).

For example, an east African washed arabica bean that's been lightly roasted can taste wildly different from an east African washed arabica bean roasted dark.

WHAT THE CUP?

When roasters want to identify flavours in coffee they use a method called cupping. This is used to check quality before buying beans, after roasting batches (to check flavours are consistent) and when combining different roasted coffees together to create blends.

1 The roaster will source a range of green bean samples and roast them to their preferred style.

SNIFFED

2 Each roasted bean sample is ground and sniffed for fragrance.

3 12g of ground coffee is added to a bowl and brewed with 200ml water at around 93°c for four minutes.

CRUST

4 The crust formed from the coffee grounds is broken using a spoon in a sweeping motion and the bloom removed from the bowl.

5 Once the coffee has cooled (after around ten minutes), it is slurped using a spoon, pulled through the mouth for tasting and often dispensed of into a spittoon (there's only so much caffeine you can manage in a day).

SLURPED

This standardised method, preparing each sample according to Specialty Coffee Association (SCA) guidelines, is used across the world. This ensures the green bean is the only variable affecting the flavour profile.

ALL IN THE SLURP

Formalities go out of the window when it comes to cupping: the bigger the slurp the better. Slurping the coffee from the spoon ensures air is also drawn up, allowing the taster to appreciate the aromas at the same time.

The tongue is actually very poor at identifying flavours (try eating a basil leaf while pinching your nose) and the art of slurping allows your brain to match the signals from your taste buds with your sense of smell for an overall perception of the taste.

CUPPING: CLUELESS TO CONNOISSEUR

While cupping was once just a tool of the trade, in recent years many speciality cafes and roasteries have opened their doors to the public and invited them to take part in after-hours cupping sessions in order to broaden their customers' coffee knowledge.

Workshops such as Dark Woods' Introduction to Coffee course guides freshers through the different influences on flavour and uses cupping as a comparative device. Ask your fave roaster or coffee shop if they've got sessions coming up and check the symbols in this guide for those running coffee courses.

SPIN THE WHEEL

While pro cuppers look for a balance of acidity, bitterness and sweetness, they're also assessing the body of the coffee and use terms such as 'buttery', 'juicy' and 'tea-like' to describe its texture.

When it comes to flavour, the SCA flavour wheel is often used to ascribe flavours in a way that will be widely understood. From vegetative to fermented, and floral to nutty, the kaleidoscope of flavours features both favoured (dark chocolate, grapefruit, hazelnut, etc) and disfavoured (rubber, ash, cardboard, etc) reference points.

Check the bag of beans in your cupboard to see what particular flavour notes are printed on it. Can you identify these flavours when you drink it?

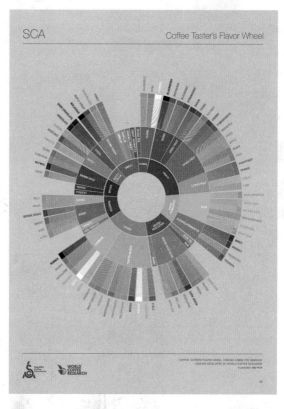

SCA — Coffee Taster's Flavor Wheel

HOW TO USE THE GUIDE

CAFES

Discover coffee shops and cafes where you can drink top-notch speciality coffee. We've divided the guide into areas to help you find places near you.

ROASTERS

Meet the leading speciality coffee roasters in the North and North Wales and discover where to source beans to use at home. Find them after the cafes in each area.

MAPS

Every member cafe and roastery has a number so you can find them either on the area map at the start of each section, or on the detailed city maps.

MORE GOOD STUFF

Explore **MORE GOOD CUPS** and **MORE GOOD ROASTERS** at the back of the book.

Don't forget to let us know how you get on as you explore the best speciality cafes and roasteries.

🐦 @indycoffeeguide

📷 @indycoffeeguide

INDYCOFFEE.GUIDE

№72
THE FLOWER CUP

NORTHUMBERLAND, TYNE AND WEAR & COUNTY DURHAM

№7
HOLMESIDE COFFEE

h

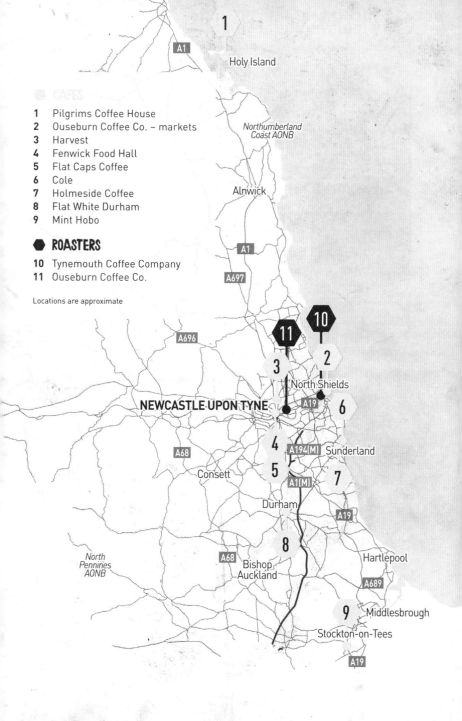

CAFES

1 Pilgrims Coffee House
2 Ouseburn Coffee Co. – markets
3 Harvest
4 Fenwick Food Hall
5 Flat Caps Coffee
6 Cole
7 Holmeside Coffee
8 Flat White Durham
9 Mint Hobo

⬢ ROASTERS

10 Tynemouth Coffee Company
11 Ouseburn Coffee Co.

Locations are approximate

MAP №

PILGRIMS COFFEE HOUSE

Falkland House, Marygate, Holy Island, Northumberland, TD15 2SJ

Pilgrims may be off the beaten track (read: over a tidal causeway only crossable by car at certain times) but this Holy Island coffee house and roastery is well worth rerouting any northern coffee tour for.

Founder Andrew Mundy and roaster Jonny bronze the house blend (Daily Bread) along with the organic Holy Grail blend and seasonal single origin offerings in a yurt within the walled gardens of the historic building. They've also started sourcing beans through a new direct trade relationship with farms in India.

TIP DON'T LEAVE WITHOUT A COPY OF PILGRIMS' OWN RECIPE BOOK, *A TASTE OF HOLY ISLAND*

The rustic roastery (ask nicely and Jonny will give you a whistlestop tour) is due to be upgraded at the end of 2018 to include room for a training space. In the meantime, ask the baristas for their tips on brewing the beans which are sold on the ground floor.

Upstairs there are plenty of cosy nooks in which to sample the house roasts as espresso or batch brew. The kitchen knocks up a stonking selection of specials and cakes if you're sticking around for lunch – just make sure you check the tide times as a day trip can easily turn into an overnighter.

ESTABLISHED
2006

KEY ROASTER
Pilgrims Coffee

BREWING METHODS
Espresso, batch brew

MACHINE
Fiorenzato San Marco, Kees van der Westen Mirage

GRINDER
Mahlkonig Peak, Mahlkonig EK43, Mahlkonig Tanzania

OPENING HOURS
Mon-Sun
9.30am-5pm
(tide permitting)

www.pilgrimscoffee.com | 01289 389109

@pilgrimscoffee   @pilgrimscoffee   @pilgrimscoffeehouse

OUSEBURN COFFEE CO. MARKETS

Tynemouth Station, Tynemouth, North Shields, Tyne and Wear, NE30 4RE

You'll still find Ouseburn Coffee Co. trading every weekend from the same patch at Tynemouth Station Market where the business started in summer 2012.

In the six years that have passed, the team have introduced batch brew to the popular stall and given customers the perfect opportunity to sample the single origin specials while picking up a bag or two of the city's freshest beans.

CAN'T MAKE IT TO THE MARKET? ORDER OCC COFFEE TO YOUR DOOR VIA THE WEBSITE

You can also try OCC's latest seasonal batch and stock up on blends for your home hopper at the monthly Monument Farmers' Market in Newcastle city centre and at Jesmond Food Market on the Victorian Armstrong Bridge every third Sunday. On the first Saturday of the month you'll find the Ouseburn crew at Gateshead's new Low Fell Food Market too.

Not sure you can keep up? Find out where the mobile market will be pitching up next – including at some of the north-east's most exciting events – via OCC's social media pages.

ESTABLISHED
2012

ROASTED
Ouseburn
Coffee Co.

BREWING METHOD
Espresso

MACHINE
Fracino

GRINDER
Sanremo

OPENING HOURS
Sat-Sun
8am-4pm

www.ouseburncoffee.co.uk   01912 707307

@ouseburncoffeeco   @ouseburncoffee   @ouseburncoffee

HARVEST

91 St George's Terrace, Jesmond, Newcastle upon Tyne, NE2 2DN

Located in the leafy suburb of Jesmond, Harvest is the flagship coffee shop from Newcastle roaster Ouseburn Coffee Co.

Serving the full OCC range of freshly roasted espresso, filter and cold brew alongside a seasonally inspired breakfast and brunch bill, it's busy with coffee folk and foodies from daybreak until late afternoon.

LIKE WHAT YOU'RE DRINKING? PICK UP A BAG OF THE SEASONAL BEANS TO-GO

The Harvest poached eggs and avocado breakfast has garnered its own fanbase in these parts, while the sumptuous selection of in-house pastries and bakes stocking the counter tempts newbies to pair something sweet with their cold-pressed juice and seasonal salad.

This year has seen the cafe open its doors – and kitchen – to guest producers and chefs who have hosted special events such as the queue-out-the-door Saturday morning pop-up bakeries.

The evening schedule featuring a monthly Friday Social has been just as popular, with everything from wood-fired pizzas to South Korean street food scoffed alongside OCC espresso martinis and craft beer.

ESTABLISHED
2014

KEY ROASTER
Ouseburn
Coffee Co.

BREWING METHOD
Espresso, V60,
AeroPress,
cold brew

MACHINE
La Marzocco
Linea PB

GRINDER
Mahlkonig EK43

OPENING HOURS
Mon-Sun
8am-6pm

www.ouseburncoffee.co.uk | 01912 707307

@ouseburncoffeeco   @ouseburncoffee   @ouseburncoffee

FENWICK FOOD HALL

39 Northumberland Street, Newcastle upon Tyne, NE1 7AS

You'll be hard pressed to find fresher coffee in the city centre than at Ouseburn Coffee Co. in Fenwick Food Hall.

The team at OCC HQ were the first to roast quality greens in Newcastle and, six years on, continue to cook ethically sourced beans in small batches from their Albion Row roastery.

TIP PICK UP A FEW BOTTLES OF HOUSE COLD BREW TO TAKE HOME

Equipped with ice-cold nitro cold brew, seasonal batch brew and a stellar house espresso, Fenwick Food Hall has everything for your post-shopping pick-me-up, including espresso martinis if you're in need of something stronger.

If you're stopping by to fortify your home supply, the stock of ethically sourced coffee can be weighed and bagged to order, and ground to your specific brewing needs.

And, if you should need help with a gift or are undecided between the seasonal single origins, the staff are always happy to offer expert advice and samples.

ESTABLISHED
2015

KEY ROASTER
Ouseburn Coffee Co.

BREWING METHOD
Espresso, nitro, cold brew

MACHINE
La Marzocco Linea PB

GRINDER
Mahlkonig EK43

OPENING HOURS
Mon-Fri
9am-8pm
Sat 9am-7pm
Sun 11am-5pm

 Gluten FREE

 BEANS AVAILABLE / INSTORE

 ALTERNATIVE MILK

 WIFI

 CYCLE FRIENDLY

 OUTDOOR seating

 FAMILY FRIENDLY

 DISABLED ACCESS

BRING YOUR OWN Cup

COFFEE COURSES

www.ouseburncoffee.co.uk   01912 707307

@ouseburncoffeeco   @ouseburncoffee   @ouseburncoffee

MAP

FLAT CAPS COFFEE

9-11 Carliol Square, Newcastle upon Tyne, NE1 6UF

Indecisive drinkers may need to schedule an extra hour for a trip to this Newcastle pioneer as the Flat Caps collection of speciality grade coffees mutates at an impressive rate.

Founder Joe Meagher was one of the first to sling speciality espresso in the city, and he continues to champion banging beans at his Newcastle hangout via a well-equipped brew bar and host of seasonal roasts from Has Bean, Workshop and Colonna.

TIP MAXED OUT ON COFFEE? CHOOSE FROM THE 15 LOOSE-LEAF TEAS

Swing by at the right time and you might also get to sample exclusive guest beans flown over by Joe's chum in Canada.

Flat Caps upped sticks to new digs on Carliol Square last year, and its combination of incredible coffee, crowd-pleasing food (try the gluten-free haggis brekkie) and light 'n' bright decor has proved so popular that opening hours have recently been extended.

The baristas continue to pull espresso (while knocking up craft cocktails) until midnight, so stick this one on your hit list under 'late-night coffee thrills'.

ESTABLISHED
2010

KEY ROASTER
Has Bean Coffee

BREWING METHOD
Espresso,
AeroPress,
Kalita Wave,
syphon

MACHINE
Sanremo
Café Racer

GRINDER
Mahlkonig Peak,
Mahlkonig EK43

OPENING HOURS
Mon-Sat
8am-12am
Sun 9am-6pm

www.flatcapscoffee.com | 01912 615748

@flatcapscoffee @flatcapscoffee @flatcapscoffee

COLE

The Side Cottage, St George's Terrace, Roker, Sunderland, Tyne and Wear, SR6 9LX

Striking up a conversation with a table neighbour is inevitable at this seaside spot as, with an espresso bar, deli counter and cluster of seating artfully squeezed into the converted front room, things can get pretty cosy at Cole.

On sunny days, the crowd of coffee lovers that come to the coast for their Climpson & Sons fix spill out onto the terrace where snug blankets and gently steaming flat whites counter the sea breeze.

PICK UP LOCAL FREE-RANGE EGGS AND A BAG OF THE BARON BLEND AT THE COUNTER

Owner Adam Cole and baker Dawn currently rustle up nearly all of the cakes and sweet thrills from home (there are plans afoot to find a bakery space), and the team prepare a surprisingly vast bill of seasonal salads, weekly toasties and topped toasts from behind the salvaged wood bar.

Even when the cafe is packed out with locals sipping batch brew and tucking into the house favourite (brie, bacon and chilli jam toastie), there's an overriding feeling of calm here. Maybe it's the salty sea air – or the much-needed dose of caffeine. We'll let you decide.

ESTABLISHED
2017

KEY DESSERT
Climpson
& Sons

BREWING METHOD
Espresso,
batch filter

MACHINE
Sanremo Zoe

GRINDER
Victoria Arduino
Mythos One

OPENING HOURS
Tue-Fri
10am-4pm
Sat-Sun
10am-5pm

 Gluten FREE

 BEANS AVAILABLE INSTORE

 ALTERNATIVE MILK

 WIFI

 OUTDOOR seating

 DISABLED ACCESS

 BRING YOUR OWN Cup

www.colecafeanddeli.co.uk   07834 236851

@colecafeanddeli   @colecafeanddeli   @colecafeanddeli

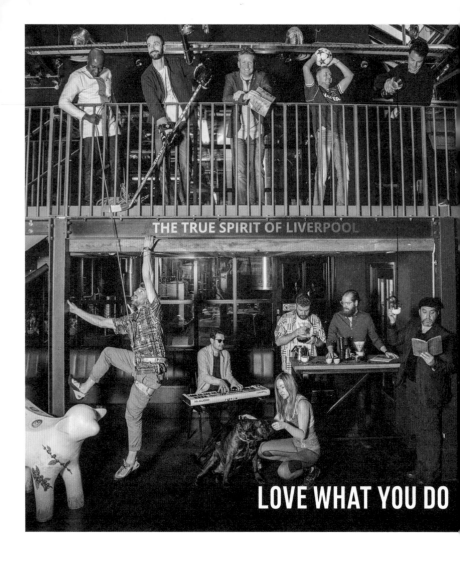

THE TRUE SPIRIT OF LIVERPOOL

LOVE WHAT YOU DO

HOLMESIDE COFFEE

Sunderland Museum & Winter Gardens, Burdon Road, Sunderland, Tyne and Wear, SR1 1PP

A slice of tropical paradise in the heart of this gritty city, Holmeside's new digs within Sunderland's Museum and Winter Gardens transport visitors to sunnier climes via its jet-setting selection of single origins and out-of-office vibes.

Multiplying its space ten-fold since moving from its nightclub/cafe hybrid, Holmeside now offers its followers the choice between cosy booth seating, tables lining the floor-to-ceiling glass rotunda and an alfresco terrace.

Newcastle-based Ouseburn Coffee provides a stellar house espresso for the cafe, with guests from the likes of Assembly and Has Bean available to try on the La Marzocco machine – as well as via batch brew.

TIP PACK AN APPETITE AS THE LUNCH SPECIALS ARE EPIC

Look out for coffee-focused events on the busy timetable of evening talks and meet-ups. *'We want to create an accessible and engaging space for ideas and quality to grow in our city,'* explains co-founder Joe Collins.

Exhibitions upstairs at the museum are always changing, so you can get a culture fix to go with your caffeine hit.

ESTABLISHED
2013

KEY ROASTER
Multiple roasters

BREWING METHOD
Espresso, batch brew

MACHINE
La Marzocco Strada EE

GRINDER
Mahlkonig EK43

OPENING HOURS
Mon-Sat 9am-5pm
Sun 10am-4pm

 Gluten FREE

 BEANS AVAILABLE / INSTORE

 ALTERNATIVE MILK

 WIFI

 CYCLE FRIENDLY

 OUTDOOR SEATING

 FAMILY FRIENDLY

 DISABLED ACCESS

 BRING YOUR OWN CUP

 COFFEE COURSES

01915 618629

f @holmesidecoffee   @holmesidecoffee   @holmesidecoffee

MAP

FLAT WHITE DURHAM

21a Elvet Bridge, Durham, DH1 3AA

It's amazing what can be achieved by two baristas hell-bent on bringing speciality culture to a city heaving with coffee chains.

After months of labouring and saving – alongside working full time jobs – Patrick Clark and Peter Anglesea turned this former Durham pizzeria into a thriving speciality hot spot that's become loved by tourists, students and locals alike.

TIP GRAB A SPOT OUTSIDE FOR ALFRESCO SIPPING

The dextrous duo still lead the team behind the coffee machine and ensure each cup is an immaculate espresso, filter or cold brew – with a little help from Newcastle roasters OCC.

But their dream didn't stop there. The cafe has also built a reputation for incredible homemade cakes and locally sourced brunches and lunches – success that has spurred Patrick and Peter to open Flat White Kitchen, a speciality-focused brunch/lunch spot on nearby Sadler Street. The five-floor mix of airy dining spaces has become the sister destination for edible adventures.

ESTABLISHED
2010

WAS ROASTED
Ouseburn Coffee Co.

BREWING METHOD
Espresso, cold brew, filter

MACHINE
La Marzocco Linea PB

GRINDER
Mazzer Robur

OPENING HOURS
Mon-Sat
9am-5pm
Sun 10am-4pm

Gluten FREE

BEANS AVAILABLE
INSTORE

ALTERNATIVE MILK

CYCLE FRIENDLY

OUTDOOR seating

www.flatwhitekitchen.com   07936 449291

@flatwhitecafedurham   @flatwhitedurham   @flatwhitedurham

MINT HOBO

30 High Street, Yarm, Stockton-on-Tees, County Durham, TS15 9AE

Whether it's a first or thirtieth trip to Yarm's lively indie coffee house, everyone is welcomed into this family fold like a long lost relative.

Day-to-day dealings at Mint Hobo have changed slightly this year as owner Steve's daughter Bethan and long-term Hobo friend Lucy have taken over. You'll often still find him chatting coffee with locals and pulling the odd espresso at this cafe in the heart of the High Street, however.

With a seven-strong selection of single origin beans from north Yorkshire roaster Rounton and an armoury of brewing gear to showcase their flavour potential, there's a lot to get bean geeks talking. If you're a fresher to speciality spiel, the team behind the bar are happy to help and will tailor a drink to your taste.

MINT'S ALL-DAY LICENCE MEANS IT'S NEVER TOO EARLY FOR AN ESPRESSO MARTINI

Repping fellow indies, Mint's simple menu of open sandwiches, toasties and glorious baked goods is stocked with ingredients from local suppliers. And if you arrive early enough, you may be able to bag one of the two-day sourdough loaves from Rise Bakehouse to accompany your flattie for the road.

ESTABLISHED
2015

KEY ROASTER
Rounton Coffee Roasters

BREWING METHODS
Espresso, V60, Chemex, syphon, cold brew

MACHINE
Sanremo Opera

GRINDER
Markibar ASPE, Mahlkonig EK43

OPENING HOURS
Mon-Sat
7am-6pm
Sun 9am-5pm

Gluten FREE

BEANS AVAILABLE INSTORE

ALTERNATIVE MILK

WIFI

CYCLE FRIENDLY

OUTDOOR seating

BRING YOUR OWN cup

COFFEE COURSES

www.minthobo.co.uk   07763 895806

@minthobo   @minthobo   @minthobo

ROADSTERS

NORTHUMBERLAND, TYNE AND WEAR & COUNTY DURHAM

MAP 10. TYNEMOUTH COFFEE COMPANY

Back Prudhoe Street, North Shields, Tyne and Wear, NE29 6RE

Home brewers keen to create a coffee-shop-style experience in the comfort of their own home make sure there's a regular delivery of Tynemouth coffee on order.

Each bag of ethically sourced beans arrives cafe-fresh, having been roasted in small batches the previous day.

The North Shields set-up is also the roaster of choice for many pro baristas, delis and restaurants across the UK – especially those who want to take their customers on a journey of discovery.

Eight quirkily named blends hint at the global adventures to be had: feel the caffeine jolt of the single origin Colombian Rocket Fuel, the brilliant blend of Colombian and Brazilian beans in the Bobby Dazzler, and the duo of South American delights in the Jingling Geordie.

'EIGHT QUIRKILY NAMED BLENDS HINT AT THE GLOBAL ADVENTURES TO BE HAD'

Tynemouth supports customers via machine supply (it stocks a range of espresso and bean-to-cup machines), training and home brew courses so everyone, from bean nerd to novice, gets to serve the best possible cup.

ESTABLISHED
2009

ROASTER
MAKE & SIZE
Toper 12kg

OPEN
BY APPOINTMENT

COFFEE COURSES

BEANS AVAILABLE
ONLINE

---

www.tynemouthcoffee.com   T: 01912 600995

f @tynemouthcoffee   **🐦** @tynemouthcoffee   **📷** @tynemouth_coffee

11. OUSEBURN COFFEE CO.

Unit 25, Albion Row, Newcastle upon Tyne, NE6 1LQ

Roasting, bagging and brewing speciality grade coffee in Newcastle since 2012, Ouseburn Coffee Co. was one of the first small batch indies in this part of the country.

The small band of passionate baristas and roasters started selling their coffee at Tynemouth Station Market the same year. While you'll still find a stall there on weekends, OCC quickly expanded to welcome two cafes and a string of producer market pitches to the fold.

As well as stocking their own family of coffee shops, the expert team roast a roll call of seasonally sourced single origins – alongside their famous Foundry blends – for a clutch of cafes and league of online customers. Highlights this year have included a new line of coffees supporting women's farming cooperatives, as well as micro lots from emerging south-east Asian and Chinese regions.

'HIGHLIGHTS THIS YEAR HAVE INCLUDED A NEW LINE OF COFFEES SUPPORTING WOMEN'S FARMING COOPERATIVES'

While OCC has temporarily closed its roastery doors to the public, trade customers are welcome to book an appointment at the Albion Row HQ.

ESTABLISHED
2012

ROASTER
MAKE & SIZE
Toper Cafemino
5kg

OPEN
BY APPOINTMENT

COFFEE COURSES

BEANS AVAILABLE
ONLINE · ONSITE

www.ouseburncoffee.co.uk   T: 01912 707307

f @ouseburncoffeeco   🐦 @ouseburncoffee   📷 @ouseburncoffee

CUMBRIA, LANCASHIRE, MERSEYSIDE & NORTH WALES

Nº14
HOMEGROUND COFFEE · KITCHEN

Locations are approximate

CAFES

25 Crosby Coffee
26 Cuppacoffee
27 Root Coffee
28 92 Degrees
29 Bean There Coffee Shop

ROASTERS

47 Crosby Coffee
48 Neighbourhood Coffee
49 The Baltic Roastery

Locations are approximate

LIVERPOOL

MAP 12.

COFFEE GENIUS

20 St Cuthberts Lane, Carlisle, Cumbria, CA3 8AG

You won't find industrial styling or neon signage at this speciality purveyor; it's the cracking coffee and award winning food that keep the caffeine lovers coming back for more.

In the past year, the Genius team have scooped a third *Carlisle Living* award for Best Cafe and have (once again) firmly cemented their place at the top of the city's coffee shop rankings.

TIP WATCH THE SYPHON MAGIC IN ACTION AT THE BREW BAR

Bean geeks with time to spare are advised to stay awhile to scoff a slice of the now famous vegan chocolate cake and enjoy the numerous brewing methods applied to the Carvetii beans – you'll need the energy load to work your way through the seven serve styles on offer.

A recent switch-up in the kitchen has refreshed the food menu and introduced stuffed savoury croissants, toasted fajita wraps and an ever-expanding selection of vegan options. Cheesecake, pavlova and decadent cream sponges are also whipped up in the Genius kitchen – and are well worth ditching the diet for.

ESTABLISHED
2014

KEY ROASTER
Carvetii Coffee Roasters

BREWING METHOD
Espresso, V60, Chemex, AeroPress, french press, filter, syphon

MACHINE
La Marzocco Linea FB80

GRINDER
Mahlkonig K30, Mahlkonig Tanzania, Mazzer Mini

OPENING HOURS
Mon-Sat
8.30am-5pm

www.coffeegenius.co.uk   01228 546594

f @coffeegenius   @coffeegenius1   @coffeegenius1

THE MOON & SIXPENCE COFFEEHOUSE

29 Main Street, Cockermouth, Cumbria, CA13 9LE

From the Cumbrian-roasted Carvetii Coffee pulled through the Marzocco machine to the locally farmed produce filling the minimalist food menu, this charming coffee shop is thoroughly rooted in its Cockermouth community.

Since opening as a coffee house in 2016, locals have even got involved by helping to stock The Moon & Sixpence's brew bar with retro cups and Denby crockery.

TIP OWNER STEPHEN BOUGHT HIS SCHOOL UNIFORM HERE BEFORE IT BECAME A CAFE

Every Thursday the friendly space doubles up as the town's farmers' market, with plump sourdough loaves and seasonal veggies pre-ordered for collection while a lively line-up of events (music and open mic nights, wine tasting, coffee cupping and fermentation workshops) brings the community together after dark.

With all this going on you'd expect coffee to be an afterthought, but the passionate baristas keep speciality standards high. Alongside the Carvetii house roast, owner Stephen likes to feature beans acquired on his travels which are fashioned into seasonal specials.

ESTABLISHED
2016

KEY ROASTER
Carvetii Coffee Roasters

BREWING METHOD
Espresso, AeroPress, batch brew

MACHINE
La Marzocco Linea PB

GRINDER
Mahlkonig K30 Air

OPENING HOURS
Mon-Sat
9am-5pm

www.the-moon-sixpence.business.site   01900 829378

@sixandmoon   @sixandmoon   @sixandmoon

HOMEGROUND COFFEE + KITCHEN

Main Road, Windermere, Cumbria, LA23 1DX

This fabulous food and speciality coffee hub in Windermere is not only a massive hit with the locals, it's also a find for caffeine fans on a tour of the lakes.

Coffee crafted in Cumbria by the guys at Carvetii provides road-trippin' tourists with a taste of the local roast, while guest beans showcase northern greats Atkinsons and Maude as well as finds from further afield such as Curve and April.

TIP
SCOUT, THE FOX RED LABRADOR PUPPY, IS HOMEGROUND'S LATEST ATTRACTION

Pick a perch at the street-facing bar for a spot of people watching, or settle down in the comfy and contemporary seating area if you're catching up with chums over coffee. Floor-to-ceiling doors at the front mean that, in summer, it's a wonderfully cool spot for an iced coffee, while in winter hunker down with a mocha.

The team are always trying out new recipes to keep things fresh, so expect daring yet delicious takes on the classics alongside well loved staples such as the (secret recipe) hash browns.

ESTABLISHED
2015

KEY ROASTER
Carvetii Coffee Roasters

BREWING METHOD
Espresso, V60, batch brew

MACHINE
La Marzocco Linea PB

GRINDER
Nuova Simonelli Mythos One

OPENING HOURS
Mon-Sun
9am-5pm

www.homegroundcafe.co.uk   01539 444863

@homegroundcafe   @homegroundcafe   @homegroundcafe

15. COMIDA [FOOD]

90 Highgate, Kendal, Cumbria, LA9 4HE

After running a bed and breakfast in Burton-in-Kendal for five years, Alba Basterra and Simon Perkin decided to trade in towels and turn-downs for tapas, and opened a bar and restaurant on Highgate.

Alba grew up in Valencia and is passionate about sharing her heritage with the local community. Curating a menu of dishes with head chef Mark Crowe that includes octopus, patatas bravas and cured meats, she crafts Spanish classics using ingredients from Basco in Harrogate.

TIP 'COMIDA' TRANSLATES AS 'FOOD' IN SPANISH

The relaxed vibe reflects the sharing nature of tapas, and this is a chilled spot in which to chat over a glass of wine or a coffee while taking time to enjoy the pared-back wood and Moorish mosaic-tiled decor.

Speciality coffee makes a perfect pairing with churros and chocolate sauce – especially the dark chocolate and hazelnut Archetype espresso roasted at nearby Atkinsons in Lancaster.

ESTABLISHED
2017

PER ROASTER
Atkinsons
Coffee Roasters

BREWING METHODS
Espresso, filter

MACHINE
Sanremo
Verona RS

GRINDER
Mythos One
Clima Pro

OPENING HOURS
Tue 12pm-late
Wed-Sat
10am-late
Sun 10am-4pm

Gluten FREE

BEANS AVAILABLE INSTORE

ALTERNATIVE MILK

WIFI

OUTDOOR seating

FAMILY friendly

DISABLED ACCESS

BRING YOUR OWN cup

www.comidafood.co.uk   01539 732082

@comidakendal   @comida_kendal   @comida_kendal

MAP№16. ATKINSONS THE MUSIC ROOM

Sun Square, Sun Street, Lancaster, Lancashire, LA1 1EW

Settle down with a filter and a fig friand on a sunny day in Lancaster and let this quiet courtyard in the centre of town become your very own secret garden.

On sunny days the cool iced coffees and luscious affogatos crafted with beans roasted (literally) over the road at Atkinsons HQ take the edge off the heat.

TIP RUGS AND 'SPROS MAKE SUN SQUARE AN OPTION ALL YEAR ROUND

On cooler visits, nab one of the handful of seats inside the buzzy Rococo-era pavilion and watch the well-trained baristas craft single origins on the trio of V60s and pull espresso through the Sanremo.

Owner, coffee guru and head honcho Ian Steel is often in and out of the micro cafe and is a fountain of speciality knowledge. Catch him – or any of the clued-up staff – for the latest tasting notes and tip-offs, as well as for tales from the team's latest trip to origin.

ESTABLISHED
2010

KEY ROASTER
Atkinsons Coffee Roasters

BREWING METHOD
Espresso, V60, batch brew

MACHINE
Sanremo Verona RS

GRINDER
Mythos One Clima Pro, Mahlkonig Tanzania

OPENING HOURS
Mon-Sat
10am-5pm
Sun 11am-4pm

 Gluten FREE

 ALTERNATIVE MILK

 WIFI

 CYCLE FRIENDLY

 OUTDOOR seating

 FAMILY FRIENDLY

 DISABLED ACCESS

 BRING YOUR OWN Cup

www.thecoffeehopper.com | 01524 65470

@themusicroomcafe   @coffeehopper   @atkinsons.coffee

ATKINSONS THE HALL

10 China Street, Lancaster, Lancashire, LA1 1EX

Despite the parade of syphons bubbling away at the bar and the rare beans celebrated on the chalkboard menu, Atkinsons' beautiful home at The Hall attracts coffee folk with all levels of knowledge.

Roasting greens before speciality became cool, owners Ian and Sue Steel know that making great coffee accessible is the key to growth in the industry, so you'll find pourover purists sharing table space with nanas having a natter over a latte.

TIP HEAD NEXT DOOR FOR ARTISAN BEANS, SPIRITS AND SINGLE ORIGIN CHOCOLATE

The whole set-up in this gorgeous old parish hall is pleasingly homemade: beans are roasted next door in the eco roastery while the house bakery crafts decadently different cakes.

Specialist drinks – including an espresso tonic, iced earl grey and New Orleans cold brew – are fresh to the summer line-up, with single origins brewed via the hypnotic syphons switching as the seasons revolve.

ESTABLISHED
2012

KEY ROASTER
Atkinsons
Coffee Roasters

BREWING METHOD
Espresso,
Chemex, syphon

MACHINE
La Marzocco
Strada EP

GRINDER
Mythos One
Clima Pro,
Mahlkonig EK43

OPENING HOURS
Mon-Sat
8am-6pm
Sun 10am-5pm

www.thecoffeehopper.com | 01524 65470

@thehallcafe   @coffeehopper   @atkinsons.coffee

MAP

EXCHANGE COFFEE COMPANY – CLITHEROE

24 Wellgate, Clitheroe, Lancashire, BB7 2DP

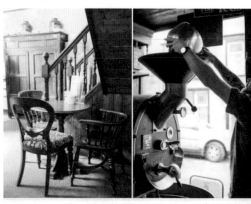

Adventurous sippers will find their curiosity pleasurably piqued at this delightful coffee house set among the indie shops of Wellgate.

Firstly there's the intrigue of the Victorian building itself. Climb the stairs to discover three unique floors where you can enjoy freshly roasted coffee plus sarnies, toasties, jacket potatoes and cakes.

Nosy home hobbyists will be intrigued to watch beans roasted on the Probat LN12 and face the dilemma of a menu of more than 35 single origin and blended coffees – not to mention 70 loose-leaf teas and tisanes.

CHECK OUT THE 1687 MARRIAGE CUPBOARD WHICH HOUSES THE ROASTED COFFEE

The Exchange team are always on the lookout for something new to excite the coffee pilgrims who congregate here, and this year they've extended their range to include (Great Taste award winning) greens from Burundi.

With all one could possibly desire in terms of brewing paraphernalia and homewares, budding brewers, inquisitive imbibers and single-origin seekers will find themselves on the path to coffee nirvana.

ESTABLISHED
1992

KEY ROASTER
Exchange Coffee Company

BREWING METHODS
Espresso, Clever Dripper, french press

MACHINE
La Marzocco GB5

GRINDER
Mahlkonig K30, Ditting KR804

OPENING HOURS
Mon-Sat
9am-5.30pm

Gluten FREE

BEANS AVAILABLE INSTORE

ALTERNATIVE MILK

WIFI

CYCLE FRIENDLY

OUTDOOR seating

FAMILY FRIENDLY

DISABLED ACCESS

BRING YOUR OWN Cup.

COFFEE COURSES

www.exchangecoffee.co.uk   01200 442270

@exchangecoffeecompany   @exchange_coffee   @exchange_coffee

№19. SHAWS

42 Clifton Street, Blackpool, Lancashire, FY1 1JP

Photo: Richard Jon Photography

Despite being a stone's skim from Blackpool's North Pier, you won't find sticks of rock or fish 'n' chips at this seaside spot – just seriously good single origin coffee and lip-smackingly great grub.

In summer, caffeine fiends flock here in search of shelter from the tourists which throng the shore, then stick around once they discover the sort of speciality gold they've stumbled upon.

Mother-and-son team Yvonne and Ryan showcase a revolving bill of European and UK roasters, with roasting greats such as Dark Arts, Curve, April, Koppi and Square Mile getting a go on the hefty collection of filter gear via an Anfim grinder.

TIP PACK YOUR KEEPCUP: IT'S A TWO MINUTE WALK FOR A BEACHSIDE SIP

The small-but-perfectly-formed foodie offering is equally inspiring. Shaws' menu takes a mostly plant-based approach with seasonal dishes including roasted Med veg, hummus and spinach bruschetta with ras el hanout dressing.

ESTABLISHED
2009

KEY ROASTER
Dark Arts Coffee

BREWING METHODS
Espresso, batch brew, AeroPress, V60, cold brew

MACHINE
La Marzocco Linea

GRINDER
Anfim Scody II

OPENING HOURS
Mon-Fri
9am-4pm
Sat 9am-3pm

 Gluten FREE

 BEANS AVAILABLE INSTORE

 ALTERNATIVE MILK

 FAMILY FRIENDLY

 DISABLED ACCESS

 COFFEE COURSES

07850 486453

@shawscafe   @shawsbpool   @shawsblackpool

TOWN HOUSE COFFEE AND BREW BAR

MAP No. 20.

62 Friargate, Preston, Lancashire, PR1 2AT

Bernice Newton had always dreamed of opening a coffee shop in her home city of Preston, but it wasn't until she'd collected the exact set of skills needed to take on the project (managing luxury hotels, bar hopping in Sydney, working on an Indian coffee plantation and helping a friend set up a cafe) that she was ready to jump.

The leap paid off and, just over a year after opening, Town House was awarded Best Independent Business 2018.

Being a part of Preston's indie hub is at the core of the sociable cafe space and Bernice supports fellow businesses, displays local artwork and hosts gigs from up-and-coming musicians.

TIP BRING YOUR POOCH ALONG – TOWN HOUSE IS SUPER DOG FRIENDLY

Sustainability is another focus at the two-storey coffee stop, with mobile flatties and homemade veggie eats leaving the shop in compostable Vegware packaging.

In line with Town House's green creds are the Resolute house beans from Origin, while single origin options from the Cornish roaster are also available to sample on the growing filter section.

ESTABLISHED
2016

KEY ROASTER
Origin Coffee Roasters

BREWING METHOD
Espresso, Chemex, cafetiere, AeroPress

MACHINE
La Marzocco Linea PB

GRINDER
Nuova Simonelli Mythos One

OPENING HOURS
Mon-Fri
8.30am-5pm
Sat 10am-4pm
Sun 11am-4pm
(seasonal opening hours)

Gluten FREE

BEANS AVAILABLE
INSTORE

ALTERNATIVE MILK

WIFI

CYCLE FRIENDLY

OUTDOOR seating

FAMILY FRIENDLY

DISABLED ACCESS

BRING YOUR OWN Cup

COFFEE COURSES

07496 421181

f @townhousecoffee62   @townhouse62   @town.house.coffee62

CEDARWOOD COFFEE COMPANY

10 Winckley Street, Preston, Lancashire, PR1 2AA

Stray from Preston's busy high street and you may just stumble upon this capsule of speciality calm at the bottom of cobbled Winckley Street.

Don't be fooled by the deceptively small downstairs set-up: in addition to the cluster of stools in the window there's a whole second floor of comfy seating and table space in which to settle down with an Atkinsons espresso.

BE SEDUCED BY A SALTED CARAMEL SHAKE WITH DOUBLE SHOT OF ESPRESSO

It's worth exploring the options before plumping for your usual, as beyond the espresso based offerings pulled through the Sanremo are cold brew and pourovers made from single origin guest beans from the likes of Red Bank.

Visiting on a hot day? Cool off with a dollop of down-the-road Wallings' luxury ice cream in one of the shakes or drenched in a shot of espresso.

Autumnal afternoons see soups, sarnies and hearty hunks of flapjack flying from the bar – or slices of gluten-free carrot cake for the (ahem) health conscious among us.

ESTABLISHED
2015

KEY ROASTER
Atkinsons
Coffee Roasters

BREWING METHOD
Espresso, V60,
cold brew

MACHINE
Sanremo Verona

GRINDER
Sanremo

OPENING HOURS
Mon-Fri
8am-5pm
Sat-Sun
11am-5pm
(seasonal
opening hours)

BEANS AVAILABLE INSTORE

ALTERNATIVE MILK

WIFI

OUTDOOR SEATING

BRING YOUR OWN Cup.

www.cedarwood.coffee 01772 821769

 @cedarwoodcoffee @winckleystreet @cedarwoodcoffee

EXCHANGE COFFEE COMPANY – BLACKBURN

13-15 Fleming Square, Blackburn, Lancashire, BB2 2DG

The irresistible aroma wafting into Fleming Square lures many a thirsty explorer of Blackburn's historic quarter into this fine stone-arched building in the Exchange Arcade.

Once inside, it's like stepping into a Victorian coffee trader's house. Fantastic old features like oak panels, an original fireplace, antique furniture and William Morris wallpaper delight the senses with a homely welcome, while the pleasing perfume of roasted-on-the-premises coffee is a potent incentive to linger.

TIP THE GUEST 1849 ESPRESSO BLEND PROVED SO POPULAR IT'S NOW A CONSTANT FIXTURE

The full Lancashire breakfast, lunches and cakes are temptation enough but the proposition of rare tasting opportunities, like trying two different varietals of Brazilian Ipanema coffee (yellow bourbon and yellow catuai) from the same estate, is even harder to refuse.

Venture upstairs to the long windowed room, sip alfresco or pop next door to the oak-panelled 1849 reading room which doubles as a private dining space.

ESTABLISHED
1986

KEY ROASTER
Exchange Coffee Company

BREWING METHOD
Espresso, AeroPress, french press

MACHINE
Cimbali M34

GRINDER
Mahlkonig K30, Ditting KR804

OPENING HOURS
Mon-Sat
9am-5.30pm

N°. 23. SIPHON ESPRESSO & BREW BAR

91 Bank Street, Rawtenstall, Rossendale, Lancashire, BB4 7QN

Rossendale's coffee-loving community couldn't believe their luck when Siphon rocked up in Rawtenstall at the start of 2018.

The speciality-sparse patch not only got a fail-safe flattie, it also benefited from a brew bar boasting V60, syphon and cold brew, and a guest line-up of north-west roasting faves.

Co-owners Scott Moore and Stuart Davies were eager to develop the coffee culture in the area and, with a little help from Ancoats in Manchester, have introduced a cracking house espresso which would turn even the most diehard of dark roast fans to the light side.

TIP PICK UP A BAMBOO CUP AND GET 10 PER CENT OFF YOUR COFFEE

Industrial-chic decor – black ceilings, wooden floors, a chipboard counter and upcycled coffee sack seats – creates a chilled-out vibe where regulars pore over their laptops or lounge in armchairs and take a little time out with friends and canine companions.

Come lunchtime, thrills come in the form of the three-cheese and red onion chutney toastie and a generous slice of homemade gluten-free banana bread.

ESTABLISHED
2018

KEY ROASTER
Ancoats Coffee Co.

BREWING METHOD
Espresso, V60, syphon, cold brew

MACHINE
Sanremo Verona RS

GRINDER
Eureka Mythos, Mazzer Mini

OPENING HOURS
Mon-Fri
7.30am-5.30pm
Sat
8.30am-5.30pm
Sun
8.30am-5pm

Gluten FREE

BEANS AVAILABLE
INSTORE

 ALTERNATIVE MILK

 WIFI

 CYCLE FRIENDLY

 OUTDOOR seating

 FAMILY friendly

 BRING YOUR OWN cup

07740 366167

 @siphonespressobrewbar   @siphonespresso1   @siphonespressobrewbar

LOVE WHAT YOU DO

Olam
Specialty
Coffee

New Name. Same Places. More great coffee.

GRIND & TAMP

45 Bridge Street, Ramsbottom, Bury, Lancashire, BL0 9AD

G uest coffees galore take centre stage at this popular speciality hangout in the heart of Ramsbottom. Headline spots on a six-strong bill of beans go to Lancaster's Atkinsons, Leeds' North Star and London's Square Mile, while a chorus of star roasters (Berlin's The Barn, Bath's Colonna and Cornwall's Origin to name a few) get a monthly moment in the spotlight.

But it's not only the coffee that will inspire a comeback tour of this charming old brick building filled with handmade reclaimed furnishings. The brunch and lunch menus change weekly and stalwarts like the sausage and egg muffin and chorizo hash have amassed their own fanbase.

LOOKING FOR A CHILLED THRILL? GUZZLE A 24-HOUR COLD BREW

Should you want to recreate your coffee experience at home, the knowledgeable team of friendly baristas offer regular espresso and pourover courses as well as cupping sessions. And you can kickstart your kitchen brew bar with a couple of bags of beans from the well-stocked retail selection.

2016

Atkinsons
Coffee Roasters

Espresso,
V60, Chemex

Sanremo
Verona RS

Mahlkonig K30,
Mythos One
Clima Pro,
Mazzer, DIP

Mon-Tue
8.30am-4pm
Thu-Sat
8.30am-4pm
Sun 10am-4pm

 Gluten FREE

 BEANS AVAILABLE INSTORE

 ALTERNATIVE MILK

WIFI

CYCLE FRIENDLY

 FAMILY FRIENDLY

 BRING YOUR OWN Cup

 COFFEE COURSES

www.grindandtampcoffee.uk   01706 558030

@grindandtampcoffee   @grind_tamp   @grind_tamp

25. CROSBY COFFEE

2 Oxford Road, Waterloo, Liverpool, Merseyside, L22 8QF

Merseyside's speciality enthusiasts have associated the name Crosby with quality coffee since Jack Foster started roasting beans from his mum's front room in 2014. And while followers could secure their fix at a handful of coffee shops and his pop-in bar, a swanky new HQ and cafe in Waterloo is bringing Crosby Coffee to the masses.

TIP 55 PER CENT BELGIAN HOT CHOCOLATE WITH BLOWTORCHED 'MALLOWS? SIGN. US. UP

With the roastery expertly bronzing a selection of ethically sourced greens next door, beans brewed at the industrial-chic bar are some of the freshest this side of the city. Choose from four seasonal coffees for espresso based drinks (two blends, a single origin and a decaf) or explore the menu of AeroPress filters, iced options and homemade cold brew.

Retail shelves climbing the exposed-brick walls are brimming with beans to take home – quiz the baristas on the tasting notes and best fit for your serve style before popping next door to watch the roasting magic in action. And if you're a brewing newbie you can sharpen your skills at one of the regular barista courses or cupping masterclasses.

ESTABLISHED
2017

KEY ROASTER
Crosby Coffee

BREWING METHOD
Espresso, AeroPress, Chemex, nitro

MACHINE
La Cimbali M34

GRINDER
Cimbali Magnum, Casadio Enea, Fiorenzato F64 Evo, Eureka Mignon

OPENING HOURS
Mon-Fri 8am-4.30pm
Sat 9am-4pm
Sun 10am-3pm

www.crosbycoffee.co.uk   01515 385454

@crosbycoffee   @coffeecrosby   @crosbycoffeeltd

CUPPACOFFEE

17 Mann Island, Liverpool, Merseyside, L3 1BP

The rabble of freelancers, creatives and office folk at Avenue HQ couldn't believe their luck when Cuppacoffee took over the ground floor of their Mann Island co-working space in 2017.

It's not just the Avenue bunch grabbing their KeepCups with glee, however: the all-weather alfresco hangout (a glass atrium brings the outside inside, 365 days a year) also provides a specialist break in the working day for Waterfront-wide desk warriors and visiting coffee buffs.

TIP THE OFF-MENU ICED COFFEE, THE BIG C, IS SWEET, CREAMY AND STRONG AS HELL

Local roaster Crosby ensures concentration levels are kept on track with a stonking three-bean blend alongside a seasonal line-up of guest roasts. Go for espresso – there's also V60 and AeroPress available – so you can watch the retro VBM lever machine in action.

Make sure you pencil a lunchtime break into your schedule too, as the sandwiches are unreal: Batman and Reuben (pastrami, swiss cheese, sauerkraut and mustard) and its veggie cousin, Sweet Baby Cheesus (cheddar, swiss cheese, sauerkraut and mustard), are as munchable as they are amusing.

ESTABLISHED
2017

KEY ROASTER
Crosby Coffee

BREWING METHOD
Espresso,
AeroPress,
pourover,
V60

MACHINE
VBM Replica
Pistone

GRINDER
Mazzer Luigi
Super Jolly

OPENING HOURS
Mon-Fri
7am-6pm
Sat-Sun
9am-5pm

 Gluten FREE

 BEANS AVAILABLE INSTORE

 ALTERNATIVE MILK

 WIFI

 CYCLE FRIENDLY

 OUTDOOR SEATING

 DISABLED ACCESS

www.cuppacoffeeuk.com   03333 153150

@cuppacoffeeuk   @cuppacoffeeuk   @cuppacoffeeuk

ROOT COFFEE

52 Hanover Street, Liverpool, Merseyside, L1 4AF

From the slick white tiles and the coffee diagrams scribbled on the blackboards it'd be easy to think that this central spot is too specialist for a casual cappuccino, but that's not the case at Root Coffee.

The baristas certainly take speciality seriously and they're more than happy to use their knowledge to recommend the best options to suit your style. Choose from a rotating roster of coffees featuring progressive European roasters – along with an armoury of filter kit – which keeps keen locals coming back to discover new faves.

With generous seating space, a friendly feel and cool decor – including a giant root hanging from the ceiling – it's easy to spend an hour here with a good book and a great coffee.

PREVIOUS GUEST FILTERS INCLUDE CASINO MOCCA, LA CABRA, RIGHT SIDE AND THE BARN

The food is worth sticking around for too. There's an ex-Michelin starred chef at the helm serving a well-priced menu, so drab lunches can be ditched in favour of Spanish canelones and pulled pork and brie piegata.

ESTABLISHED
2015

KEY ROASTER
Multiple roasters

BREWING METHODS
Espresso, Chemex, cold brew, V60

MACHINE
Victoria Arduino Black Eagle Gravimetric

GRINDER
Mythos One Clima Pro

OPENING HOURS
Mon-Sat 8.30am-6.30pm
Sun 9am-6pm

www.rootcoffee.co.uk

@rootcoffeeliv   @rootcoffeeliv   @rootcoffeeliv

92 DEGREES

24 Hardman Street, Liverpool, Merseyside, L1 9AX

Liverpool's first combined coffee shop and roastery has been roasting and extracting the freshest coffee in the north-west since 2015, when five friends set up shop on the corner of Hope and Hardman Streets.

It's as serious about good coffee as its name (the optimum temperature for espresso extraction according to the team) suggests, though you won't find any guest roasters on the menu here as all beans are bronzed in house. Try the house blend, Hope Street Espresso, in a flattie or, for a cleaner cup, plump for one of the single origins via V60.

SAVE THE PLANET AND 10 PER CENT OFF TAKEAWAYS WITH A 92 DEGREES KEEPCUP

Home brew hobbyists can also pick up kit (gear and beans) to craft their fave 92 Degrees coffee at home.

However, it's all too tempting to simply nab a spot on the communal bench (or collapse into one of the leather sofas) and let someone else do the coffee crafting while you enjoy lunch and the collectively crafted playlist.

Locals can also bag themselves a bargain as the cafe offers various discounts through the Independent Liverpool Card and Colu.

ESTABLISHED
2015

KEY ROASTER
92 Degrees Coffee

BREWING METHODS
Espresso, V60, cold brew

MACHINE
Expobar Diamant

GRINDER
Mazzer Luigi SRL

OPENING HOURS
Mon-Fri 7.45am-7pm
Sat 9.30am-7pm
Sun 10am-6pm

 Gluten FREE

 BEANS AVAILABLE INSTORE

 ALTERNATIVE MILK

 WIFI

 CYCLE FRIENDLY

 OUTDOOR seating

 FAMILY FRIENDLY

 DISABLED ACCESS

 BRING YOUR OWN Cup

COFFEE COURSES

www.92degreescoffee.com   01517 091145

@92degreescoffee   @92degreescoffee   @92degreescoffee

BEAN THERE COFFEE SHOP

MAP №. 29.

376 Smithdown Road, Liverpool, Merseyside, L15 5AN

A year on since being inspired to introduce speciality to their south Liverpool patch, Andrew and Candice Mulligan celebrated Bean There's first birthday in style by securing an alcohol licence and launching a boozy bill of caffeine-infused cocktails.

With extended opening hours and a good selection of craft beer and wine, evening visits to this speciality palace can be toasted with tea-spiked G&Ts and espresso martinis, while daytime drop-ins are an opportunity to pore over silky flat whites and doorstop slices of Cakesmiths traybakes.

TIP WEEKLY LIVE MUSIC AND OTHER EVENTS MEAN THE PLACE IS ALWAYS BUZZING

Lancaster's Atkinsons Coffee Roasters is the house fave, alongside a roster of guests on filter; just let the friendly staff know what you're into and they'll be on it with the latest tasting notes.

Mingling with the aroma of freshly brewed coffee is the waft of hot-from-the-oven soda bread and homemade sausage rolls – meat, veggie and vegan – courtesy of the Bean There kitchen. Grab a brew and some grub and settle in among the rabble of laptop tappers, feasting families and caffeine-hungry office folk.

ESTABLISHED
2017

KEY ROASTER
Atkinsons
Coffee Roasters

BREWING METHOD
Espresso, V60,
Chemex,
batch brew

MACHINE
La Marzocco
Linea PB

GRINDER
Mythos One
Clima Pro,
Mahlkonig EK43

OPENING HOURS
Mon-Wed
7.30am-6pm
Thu-Fri
7.30am-9.30pm
Sat 9am-9.30pm
Sun 9am-5pm

 Gluten FREE

 BEANS AVAILABLE / INSTORE

 ALTERNATIVE MILK

 WIFI

 OUTDOOR seating

 FAMILY friendly

 DISABLED ACCESS

 BRING YOUR OWN Cup

www.beantherecoffeeshop.com   01517 332324

f @beantherecoffeeshop   @beanthere_lpl   @beantherecoffeeshop

CAFFÈ & CO.

8 Dane Court, Rainhill, Prescot, Merseyside, L35 4LU

Fashioning filter before the first wisps of hair appeared on most current hipsters' top lips, Caffè & Co. can lay claim to being one of the first speciality shops in the north-west.

Instead of opting for a city spot, owner Neil Osthoff chose the relatively small village of Rainhill from which to craft incredible brews – perfect for those seeking good coffee with a side of peace and quiet. Find your place among the families, friends and couples who frequent this roomy cafe for an expertly prepared cup of Extract or Union coffee.

TIP HOT DAY? COOL OFF WITH AN ICE CREAM FROM THE MIGHTY ARRAY OF FLAVOURS

With three single origins from guests such as Gardelli and Artisan Roast available on filter at any time, espresso heads are often turned in favour of something slow. We'd recommend perusing the drool-inducing menu – including a cracking line-up of veggie goodies – while you wait for your drink from the brew bar.

Bean freak? Hotfoot it upstairs for a glimpse of the barista alchemy going down at the SCA-approved coffee training school.

ESTABLISHED
2011

KEY ROASTER
Multiple roasters

BREWING METHOD
Espresso,
AeroPress,
Clever Dripper,
Chemex, V60

MACHINE
La Marzocco
Linea PB,
La Marzocco GB5

GRINDER
Victoria Arduino
Mythos One

OPENING HOURS
Mon-Fri
8.30am-4.30pm
Sat 9am-4.30pm
Sun
10.30am-2.30pm

Gluten FREE

BEANS AVAILABLE INSTORE

ALTERNATIVE MILK

WIFI

CYCLE FRIENDLY

OUTDOOR SEATING

FAMILY FRIENDLY

DISABLED ACCESS

BRING YOUR OWN CUP

COFFEE COURSES

www.caffeandco.com   01514 932332

Caffè & Co.   caffeandco   caffe_and_co

MAP №

KING STREET COFFEE COMPANY

1 Lord Street Arcade, Wrexham, North Wales, LL11 1LF

Brothers Phil and Andy Gallanders have been flying the caffeinated flag in Wrexham since 2016, and show no sign of any impending coffee come-down.

In fact the bean bros have been rather busy and, in addition to opening a second coffee site, Blank Canvas, have also launched craft beer bar, Bank Street Social, around the corner.

TIP CHECK OUT THE OVER-ICE OFFERING WHEN THE TEMPERATURE ROCKETS

You'll find the original KSCC at Wrexham Bus Station, making it the perfect place to sip a batch brew if you've missed your ride or got a lengthy wait for the next wagon. Grab a slab of vegan orange pistachio cake to pair with your Neighbourhood beans and time will fly.

Stuffed with puns, the cafe's social media is as cheesy as the oozing toasties on the menu (it also fully embraces #coffeeporn). It's all quite fitting of the pair, who state their motto is *'serving great coffee and tea without taking ourselves too seriously.'*

Helping to improve Wrexham is also a cause close to Phil and Andy's hearts; you'll find the King Street squad at local events and collaborating with other indies.

ESTABLISHED
2016

ROASTER
Neighbourhood Coffee

BREWING METHOD
Espresso, batch brew

MACHINE
Sanremo Verona RS

GRINDER
Macap MXD

OPENING HOURS
Mon-Fri
7am-5pm
Sat 8.30am-4pm

Gluten FREE

BEANS AVAILABLE
INSTORE

ALTERNATIVE MILK

WIFI

DISABLED ACCESS

BRING YOUR OWN Cup.

www.kingstreetcoffee.co.uk   01978 448818

@kingstreetcoffeecompany   @kingstcoffee   @kingstcoffeecompany

BL_NK C_NV_S

Tŷ Pawb, Market Street, Wrexham, North Wales, LL13 8BY

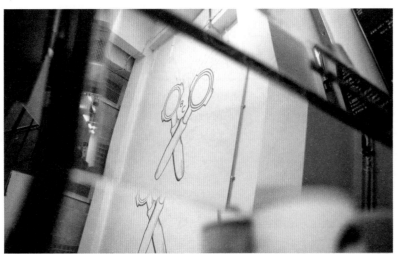

Wrexham's spankingly new community hub, Tŷ Pawb (translating as 'everybody's house'), has provided a buzzy central spot for the North Wales town. And between its art galleries, performance space, traditional market stalls and food court, you'll find an outpost from the brothers behind King Street Coffee Company.

With a sweet patch close to one of the entrances, the Blank Canvas team are self-appointed hosts to Tŷ Pawb. They take their job of welcoming the punters seriously, providing quality at the outset of the visitor experience with kickass espresso drinks and filter brews via the La Marzocco machine, batch brewer and AeroPress.

PICK UP A LOCALLY BAKED CAKE TO MUNCH AS YOU WANDER THE MARKET STALLS

Liverpool-roasted beans can be savoured in peace at the slick white space (complete with espresso mural by local tattoo artist Tommy Clayton), or return when one of the lively series of activities is taking place: *'Whether it's a community art club, choir practice or international music festival, there's always something different going on,'* smiles co-owner Phil Gallanders.

2018

Neighbourhood Coffee

Espresso, batch brew, AeroPress

La Marzocco Linea PB

Victoria Arduino Mythos One

Mon-Fri
8am-5pm
Sat 9am-4.30pm
Sun 10am-4pm

www.typawb.wales   07450 518635

@blankcanvaswrexham   @blankcanvaswxm   @blankcanvaswrexham

great **taste** PRODUCER

Award Winning
Handmade Cakes

Lemon & Courgette Loafcake

CAKESMITHS
CAKES FOR COFFEE SHOPS

cakesmithsHQ #Cakesmiths.HQ @CakesmithsHQ

PROVIDERO – LLANDUDNO

112 Upper Mostyn Street, Llandudno, Conwy, North Wales, LL30 2SW

Fellow startups followed Jon Hughes' lead when he chose Upper Mostyn hill for Providero's second outpost, which kickstarted an indie hub a pebble's skim from Llandudno's shoreside centre.

The sociable space is the uncut version of the original coffee shop at Llandudno Junction, and features a meatier food menu, extended weekend opening hours and the first Sanremo Opera espresso machine to grace a Welsh bar.

LOOK OUT FOR CUPPING SESSIONS WITH HEARTLAND

As the guys at Heartland roast the house beans a mere ten minute walk across town, Jon is able to drop into the roastery a couple of times a week to cup new coffees and tweak espresso recipes. Northern neighbours Atkinsons, Heart and Graft and Neighbourhood also feature from time to time on the single estate guest spot.

Keen to make the cafe as eco-friendly as possible, Jon has introduced fully compostable cups and straws, and works to ensure waste is kept to a minimum. Make sure to pack a Tupperware if you're grabbing one of the colourful salads or freshly layered sandwiches to-go.

ESTABLISHED
2017

KEY ROASTER
Heartland
Coffee Roasters

BREWING METHOD
Espresso,
AeroPress,
Clever Dripper,
filter

MACHINE
Sanremo Opera

GRINDER
Mythos One
Clima Pro,
Mahlkonig EK43

OPENING HOURS
Mon-Sat
8am-6pm
Sun 9am-5pm

 Gluten FREE

 BEANS AVAILABLE INSTORE

 ALTERNATIVE MILK

WiFi

 CYCLE FRIENDLY

 OUTDOOR seating

 FAMILY FRIENDLY

 DISABLED ACCESS

 BRING YOUR OWN Cup

www.providero.co.uk   01492 338220

@providero   @providero   @providero.tea.coffee

MAP

PROVIDERO – LLANDUDNO JUNCTION

148 Conway Road, Llandudno Junction, Conwy, North Wales, LL31 9DU

This lovable little coffee shop at Llandudno Junction is affectionately known to the locals as Little Prov.

Although not actually the smallest member of the Providero family – owner Jon Hughes founded the speciality project via a converted Citroën van circa 2010 – the compact cafe space earned the new nickname when its big sister shop opened in Llandudno in 2017.

The original bricks-and-mortar cafe specialises in brewing incredible coffee with beans from Heartland – as well as guests such as Heart and Graft and Neighbourhood – and selling retail bags and coffee gear for fans to take home.

MISSED BREKKIE? GRAB A SLICE OF BUTTERY DOORSTEP TOAST WITH CONWY JAM

Settle in a cosy nook upstairs among the bookshelves and treat yo'self to a slice of something rich 'n' sticky from the bake alchemists at Cakesmiths.

There's no kitchen and the team are super laid back so feel free to take your lunch along if you're calling in for a brew (the team also bang out a luscious luxe hot choc and speciality teas).

ESTABLISHED
2014

KEY ROASTER
Heartland
Coffee Roasters

BREWING METHODS
Espresso,
AeroPress,
Clever Dripper,
batch brew

MACHINE
La Marzocco
Linea PB

GRINDER
Mythos One
Clima Pro,
Mahlkonig EK43

OPENING HOURS
Mon-Fri
8am-5pm
Sat 9am-5pm
Sun 10am-4pm

Gluten FREE

BEANS AVAILABLE INSTORE

ALTE RNA TIVE MILK

WIFI

DISABLED ACCESS

BRING YOUR OWN Cup

www.providero.co.uk   01492 338220

@providero   @providero   @providero.junction

MAP 36. CARVETII COFFEE ROASTERS

Threlkeld Business Park, Threlkeld, Cumbria, CA12 4SU

Carvetii's combination of contemporary roasting and traditional customer service is certainly paying off. Last year the team expanded their premises and invested in a new 25kg Probat roaster to meet the demand for their Cumbrian-roasted beans.

Typically, there are six coffees on the go at any one time: a classic seasonal espresso blend, which usually showcases African beans; a Knott Halloo espresso blend with less acidity; three single origins for filter and a decaf option.

Two new training rooms allow the gang to teach professionals, tradespeople and home brewers how to improve their skills and boost their understanding of the processes involved. Carvetii is one of only a few SCA-accredited trainers in the north-west.

ESTABLISHED
2011

ROASTER
MAKE & SIZE
Probatone 25kg
Probat UC12
12kg

OPEN
BY APPOINTMENT

COFFEE COURSES

COURSES

BEANS AVAILABLE

ONLINE

'CARVETII IS ONE OF ONLY A FEW SCA-ACCREDITED TRAINERS IN THE NORTH-WEST'

For those in the industry, it's also worth noting that the roastery sells, leases, repairs, maintains and services a range of professional equipment. For those who simply love good coffee, find Carvetii's beans in cafes across the Lake District, sign up for a monthly subscription or book onto a roastery tour.

www.carvetiicoffee.co.uk   T: 01768 776979

f @Carvetii Coffee   🐦 @carvetiicoffee   📷 @carvetiicoffee

№37. RED BANK COFFEE ROASTERS

Unit 3a, Lake Road Estate, Lake Road, Coniston, Cumbria, LA21 8EW

A move to a roomier roastery at the start of 2018 has already resulted in some exciting opportunities for Red Bank.

The Coniston roastery has recently been appointed as a La Marzocco distributor, while more space has facilitated the upsizing of the roaster to a Loring S15 Falcon. This impressive piece of kit joins the 6kg Giesen in roasting a deliciously diverse range of beans sourced from some of the best ethical coffee farms around the world.

Owner Tom Prestwich has also launched a comprehensive barista training facility with new recruit Mike Dickinson, with plans to offer SCA-accredited courses from 2019.

'OWNER TOM PRESTWICH HAS ALSO LAUNCHED A COMPREHENSIVE BARISTA TRAINING FACILITY'

A pop-up cafe adds another new notch to the Red Bank belt this year – check social media to find out when the baristas are slinging shots.

If you can't make it to the swanky new digs, a nifty letterbox subscription service delivers a variety of coffees in specially designed bags direct to your door.

ESTABLISHED
2015

ROASTER
MAKE & SIZE
Loring S15
Falcon 15kg
Giesen W6A 6kg

CAFE ONSITE

OPEN BY APPOINTMENT

COFFEE COURSES

BEANS AVAILABLE
ONLINE ONSITE

---

www.redbankcoffee.com   T: 07850 291171

f @redbankcoffee   🐦 @redbankroasters   @redbankcoffee

38. MR DUFFINS COFFEE

49 Main Street, Staveley, Kendal, Cumbria, LA8 9LN

What began as a friend's foodie challenge led to roaster Steven Duffin's obsession with creating the ultimate brew. This, in turn, kickstarted a successful family business.

Steven's roasting journey began at home with a 2kg Brazilian roaster bought on eBay but, as demand grew and the orders started to roll in, Mr Duffin needed roomier premises and a meatier machine.

Now a gleaming 15kg Giesen takes pride of place in his Staveley coffee shop, The Coffee Den, where you can watch the beans browning twice a week as you sample a cup and tuck into a slice of something sweet.

ESTABLISHED
2014

ROASTER
MAKE & SIZE
Giesen 15kg

'ROASTING JUST BEFORE POSTING ENSURES THE FRESHEST COFFEE EXPERIENCE'

Always innovating and experimenting, Steven and wife Eleanor source beans from all over the globe to produce delectable single origin coffees as well as perfectly balanced blends like new Chin Wag (medium bodied with notes of toasted nuts and a milk chocolate finish).

Beans are sold on site and online, and roasting just before posting ensures the freshest coffee experience. Brewing equipment, artisan chocolate, specialist tea and a selection of gifts are also available online.

www.mrduffinscoffee.com   T: 01539 822192

f @Mr Duffins Coffee   🐦 @mrduffins   📷 @mr.duffins.coffee

№:39. RINALDO'S SPECIALITY COFFEE & FINE TEA

Unit 12, Lakeland Food Park (Plumgarths), Kendal, Cumbria, LA8 8QJ

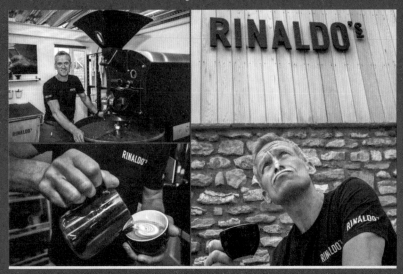

Upping sticks to a brand new EU-funded roastery in December 2017, Rinaldo's has taken its speciality operation up a notch to include a comprehensive training centre and espresso bar.

Inviting burgeoning home brewers and wannabe baristas to the Cumbrian base on Saturdays, founder Rin Colombi now offers bespoke courses to cover everything from latte art to brewing techniques.

'RIN IS SUPER APPROACHABLE AND ALWAYS UP FOR A CHAT ABOUT WHAT HE'S GOT IN THE GIESEN'

Whether you're dropping by to pick up beans for the home hopper, taking part in the introductory barista workshop or hitting the espresso bar for a quick shot, Rin is super approachable and always up for a chat about what he's got in the Giesen.

A typical week will see a seasonal single origin and the house Casa Espresso blend browning in the 15kg roaster. Rin also blends an organic half caf which still packs a punch for those craving a coffee after dinner, and throws in free delivery for customers in the local area.

ESTABLISHED
2015

ROASTER
MAKE & SIZE
Giesen W15
15kg

CAFE ONSITE

OPEN TO THE PUBLIC

COFFEE COURSES

BEANS AVAILABLE
ONLINE ONSITE

---

www.rinscoffee.com T: 01539 592587

f @rinscoffee   🐦 @rinscoffee   📷 @rinscoffee

MAP 40. FARRER'S TEA & COFFEE

9 Shap Road Industrial Estate, Kendal, Cumbria, LA9 6NZ

One of the early pioneers in UK coffee roasting, the team behind Farrer's are stockpiling banners and polishing their dance shoes ahead of their bicentenary anniversary celebrations in 2019.

Producing more than 50 blends and single origin coffees with beans sourced from El Salvador to Ethiopia and beyond over the years, Farrer's commitment has long been to provide customers with the very best coffee.

That means not only importing the best beans and roasting them to exacting standards, but also imparting training and knowledge to guarantee each batch is brewed to its optimum potential.

ESTABLISHED
1819

ROASTER
MAKE & SIZE
Probat G60 60kg
Vittoria 15kg
Probatino 1.5kg

OPEN
BY APPOINTMENT

COFFEE
COURSES

BEANS
AVAILABLE
ONLINE   ONSITE

'PRODUCING MORE THAN 50 BLENDS AND SINGLE ORIGIN COFFEES WITH BEANS SOURCED FROM EL SALVADOR TO ETHIOPIA'

For those who appreciate a great bit of coffee kit when they see it, Farrer's recently revamped showroom at its Kendal HQ boasts a new Café Racer and Zoe Vision from Sanremo alongside other gleaming machines.

Book yourself in for a roastery tour or, better still, hone your barista skills at one of the coffee school courses.

---

www.farrerscoffee.co.uk   T: 01539 720020

f @farrersteaandcoffee   🐦 @farrers_coffee   📷 @farrersteaandcoffee

MAP 41. KIRCABI ROASTERS

The Royal Barn, New Road, Kirkby Lonsdale, Cumbria, LA6 2AB

A combination of local heritage and international influence marks Kircabi as a roaster with characterful quirks to be uncovered.

The Toper was recently packed up and moved to a new home at The Royal Barn. *'It's a unique building steeped in history,'* says owner Stu Taylor. These roots are key to the indie set-up's identity: Kircabi is the Old Norse spelling of Kirkby, after all.

'THE TURKISH COPPER TOPER IS A SIGHT TO BEHOLD'

Local links mingle with the exotic in the striking showpiece roaster. The Turkish copper Toper is a sight to behold when bronzing greens from around the globe – which explains the crowd often found lingering at the in-house cafe (long after they've finished their brew) in order to ogle the roasting taking place.

Small batch beans are carefully crafted using ethically procured harvests from across Africa, India, Indonesia and the Americas. Every batch comes with info on the region and farmer that the coffee came from, so sippers can read the sustainable story behind each cup.

ESTABLISHED
2016

ROASTER
MAKE & SIZE
Toper 5kg

CAFE ONSITE

OPEN BY APPOINTMENT

BEANS AVAILABLE
ONLINE ONSITE

---

www.kircabiroasters.co.uk   T: 01524 271918

f @kircabi   🐦 @kircabiroasters   📷 @kircabiroasters

MAP 42. ATKINSONS COFFEE ROASTERS

12 China Street, Lancaster, Lancashire, LA1 1EX

Whether it's tales of chucking rocks at firecrackers in Colombia or relics from a road trip around Nicaragua, Atkinsons' owner and head roaster Ian Steel always has a good story to tell about his latest expedition to origin.

'Meeting the farmers who supply our beans allows us to build relationships – and we've been able to see the quality of their beans develop year by year,' explains Ian.

Back home in Lancaster's coffee quarter, Ian and the team pull together to supply not only their own trio of cafes with roasted and rested beans, but also hundreds of other specialist outlets across the region. The small tribe of machines roast a range of batch sizes almost every day and visitors are always welcome to have a peek inside the roastery behind the shop.

'MEETING THE FARMERS WHO SUPPLY OUR BEANS ALLOWS US TO BUILD RELATIONSHIPS'

However, you don't need to visit to get an Atkinsons fix as its letterbox-friendly subscriptions are super efficient and have just extended to include an office service. Fans can also catch up on the team's latest globetrotting trips and meet the farmers behind the latest single origin beans via the online journal.

ESTABLISHED
1837

ROASTER
MAKE & SIZE
Loring Kestrel 35kg
Whitmee 56lb
Whitmee 28lb
Uno 14lb

---

www.thecoffeehopper.com   T: 01524 65470

f @atkinsonscoffee   🐦 @coffeehopper   📷 @atkinsons.coffee

MAP Nº 43. POCOESPRESSO

29 The Gables, Cottam, Preston, Lancashire, PR4 0LG

This fresh face on the Lancashire scene may be micro ('poco' meaning 'little' in Italian) but it delivers big on flavour.

'Coffee starts to lose its flavour within ten minutes of grinding, and no amount of fancy storage can stop it,' says roaster and co-owner Lewis Duffy. That's why he and dad Steve run a whole-bean-focused affair with their sublimely sippable single origins from across the globe.

They're a personable pair: *'Coffee is about relationships – whether meeting friends for a catch up over a brew or working closely with the people who grow and harvest the coffee,'* says Steve. So you'll find them meticulously striving to create a personal experience for their customers, from home coffee connoisseurs to machine manufacturers.

'COFFEE IS ABOUT RELATIONSHIPS'

From crafting a specific La Pavoni-approved blend to creating batch and cold brew solutions for cafes, this Preston father-and-son duo are on the verge of something big.

ESTABLISHED
2017

ROASTER
MAKE & SIZE
Dongyi 2kg

COFFEE COURSES

BEANS AVAILABLE

ONLINE

---

www.pocoespresso.com   T: 07488 353375

f @pocoespresso   🐦 @pocoespresso   📷 @pocoespresso

MAP: 44. EXCHANGE COFFEE COMPANY

The Old Baptist Chapel, Islington, Canterbury Street, Blackburn, Lancashire, BB2 2LN

This hallowed spot is where the speciality congregation of Blackburn gather to learn about the almighty bean.

Exchange Coffee Company has its own barista training facility in the old Sunday school of its converted 1764 baptist chapel and, for those who worship great coffee, it's a heavenly location in which to train.

A holy trinity of roasters (two Petroncini and a Probat GN25) sanctify coffees from more than 15 countries. Sourcing single estate and Rainforest Alliance beans, the roasting team are also excited about working with new micro lots from the likes of Burundi International Women's Coffee Alliance.

'THE JOY IS THAT WE LEARN SOMETHING NEW ABOUT COFFEE EVERY SINGLE DAY'

The roastery, which has won 37 Great Taste awards, works closely with Cimbali and Expobar to offer coffee shops the full package: installing and servicing machines and providing advice and training.

The Exchange experience has become synonymous with divine brews across the region and you'll find its roasting shop in Fleming Square and coffee bar in Blackburn Market.

ESTABLISHED
1996

ROASTER
MAKE & SIZE
Petroncini TTA
60 60kg
Probat GN25
25kg
Petroncini TTA
15/20 20kg

OPEN
BY APPOINTMENT

BEANS
AVAILABLE
ONLINE   ONSITE

---

www.exchangecoffee.co.uk   T: 01254 781560

f @exchangecoffeecompany   🐦 @exchange_coffee   📷 @exchange_coffee

№45. ROBERTS & CO.

Cedar Farm, Back Lane, Mawdesley, Ormskirk, Lancashire, L40 3SY

The Roberts family are no strangers to roasting: they've been bronzing beans since the 1930s.

Since 1989, the family have been based at a former pig farm, Cedar Farm, where their roasting HQ forms part of a bustling countryside community of like-minded indies.

In the heart of bucolic Lancashire, they not only craft single origin beans and house blends but continue the family business of trading in quality tea.

Customers are invited to buy beans online or visit the roastery, where there's an opportunity to sip a brew at the espresso bar and watch the "industrial antique" Whitmee roasters firing up.

'THE ROASTING HQ IS PART OF A BUSTLING COUNTRYSIDE COMMUNITY OF LIKE-MINDED INDIES'

Swing by for beans at lunchtime and make it the perfect excuse to visit nearby Cedar Farm Cafe (also owned by the family) for local and seasonal specials.

ESTABLISHED
1891

ROASTER
MAKE & SIZE
Vintage
Whitmee 20kg
Vintage
Whitmee 6kg

CAFE ONSITE

BEANS AVAILABLE
ONLINE ONSITE

www.e-coffee.co.uk   T: 01704 822433
f @Roberts & Co Roastery   @ @robertsco_coffee

46. DJANGO COFFEE CO.

24 Kenilworth Road, Ainsdale, Southport, Merseyside, PR8 3PE

Inspired by globetrotting adventures and a stint in the third wave coffee capital of Melbourne, Django's socially conscious roastery is cooking up a supersonic selection of beans for its loyal legion of subscribers.

Partnering with suppliers who share the same ethics of trust, transparency and integrity, owner and roaster Stephen Paweleck sources greens from across Latin America and Africa. He's also been experimenting with beans from Myanmar and China.

The seasonally shifting selection of single origins earned Django a spot on *The Independent*'s Top Seven Subscriptions list. And if you're looking to join in, novice baristas will find a helpful collection of brewing guides on the website for the perfect serve.

'THE SELECTION OF COFFEES EARNED DJANGO A SPOT ON THE INDEPENDENT'S TOP SEVEN SUBSCRIPTIONS'

As well as ensuring a fair price goes to its farmers, the roastery strives to reduce its environmental impact. *'We want to roast amazing coffee while minimising our footprint on the environment and making sure that each stage of the coffee chain is carried out with an understanding that does justice to everyone involved,'* explains Stephen.

ESTABLISHED
2016

ROASTER
MAKE & SIZE
Giesen W6A 6kg

BEANS AVAILABLE
ONLINE ONSITE

---

www.djangocoffeeco.com   T: 07490 387610

f @djangocoffeeco   🐦 @djangocoffee   📷 @djangocoffeeco

47. CROSBY COFFEE

2 Oxford Road, Waterloo, Liverpool, Merseyside, L22 8QF

The tight team behind Crosby Coffee moved their busy roastery from a small industrial unit to a spacious shop this year, launching their first bricks-and-mortar cafe and allowing their loyal following a closer peek at the roasting process.

At the new Waterloo HQ, enthusiasts can sample the latest single origin coffees and house blends fresh from the Toper, while watching green beans carefully brown in the sample roaster. They can also get hands-on at cupping classes in the dedicated training room.

ESTABLISHED
2014

ROASTER
MAKE & SIZE
Toper 10kg

'GET HANDS-ON AT CUPPING CLASSES IN THE DEDICATED TRAINING ROOM'

Sourcing from coffee farms in Malawi, Honduras, Costa Rica and Colombia, co-owners Jack and Mark refresh the single origin offering on a monthly basis, which they then supply to a wealth of local coffee shops and home brewers through subscription packages.

Having garnered a healthy collection of silverware already, including Producer of the Year 2016 and Favourite Place to Shop 2017, it probably won't be long before this new venture also brings home a trophy or two.

www.crosbycoffee.co.uk   **T:** 01515 385454

f @crosbycoffee   🐦 @coffeecrosby   📷 @crosbycoffeeltd

^{MAP №}48. NEIGHBOURHOOD COFFEE

Unit 89, Chadwick Court, Chadwick Street, Liverpool, Merseyside, L3 7EY

ince launching in 2014 as Liverpool's first speciality roastery, Neighbourhood Coffee has flourished like a vibrant coffee bush heavy with cherries.

Neighbourhood's team of five believe that coffee tastes better when it's fresh, so they roast beans by hand in small lots almost every day, sampling along the way to ensure each batch is exemplary.

It's an experienced team – founders Chris and Ed worked for many years for a major green bean importer – and they are all focused on total transparency about the process, from sourcing to roasting and brewing. Interested parties are welcome to book a visit to the roastery or take a training class.

With direct relationships with farmers in Brazil, Guatemala and Ethiopia, Neighbourhood is also making progress with community development projects in the areas it sources from.

ESTABLISHED
2014

ROASTER
MAKE & SIZE
Giesen W15A
15kg

OPEN
BY APPOINTMENT

COFFEE
COURSES

COURSES

BEANS
AVAILABLE
ONLINE ONSITE

NEIGHBOURHOOD'S NEW CAFE, FRAMEWORK COFFEE, LAUNCHES AUTUMN 2018

The crew also procures micro lots from Guatemala (La Loma, Finca Villaure) and Brazil (Jacutinga), plus seasonal specials and subscription-only coffees.

---

www.neighbourhoodcoffee.co.uk   T: 01512 366741

f @neighbourhoodcoffee   🐦 @nhoodcoffee   📷 @neighbourhoodcoffee

MAP Nᵒ 49. THE BALTIC ROASTERY

49 Jamaica Street, Liverpool, Merseyside, L1 0AF

The crew behind 92 Degrees are pumped to have joined the city's Baltic Triangle creative community following an expansion to new and bigger premises.

Their longstanding passion and enthusiasm for coffee has had an influence on everything in the new endeavour, and the team are bubbling over with excitement to be a part of the up-and-coming quarter: *'It's a converted old warehouse. Not historic red brick, concrete and steel lintels – but just as awesome.'*

Phase one involved a pop-up coffee shop (complete with Faema E71 machine), and phase two includes developing the roasting operation at Jamaica Street. In addition to more roasting room, the team have installed a full service kitchen, so brunch and evening dishes are being served alongside own-roasted brews.

'92 DEGREES ARE PUMPED TO HAVE JOINED THE CITY'S BALTIC TRIANGLE CREATIVE COMMUNITY'

And, of course, bean geeks can still visit the clan's original outpost (and the city's first roastery cafe) on the corner of Hardman Street.

ESTABLISHED
2015

ROASTER
MAKE & SIZE
Giesen W6A 6kg
Diedrich 2.5kg

CAFE ONSITE

OPEN BY APPOINTMENT

BEANS AVAILABLE
ONLINE ONSITE

T: 01517 091145
@thebalticroastery

MAP № 50. HEARTLAND COFFEE ROASTERS

Unit 6, Cwrt Roger Mostyn, Builder Street, Llandudno, North Wales, LL30 1DS

It's all change at Malcolm Klose's North Wales roastery. Since moving across the courtyard to a roomier spot in summer 2018, Heartland has been able to open its doors to the coffee curious.

Installing a chunky 45kg Coffee-Tech Ghibli to meet increasing demand, and introducing a mezzanine-level coffee shop in which customers can sip the home-bronzed bounty, Heartland's fresh set-up has cemented the roastery's reputation as one of the major players on the northern scene.

Beans landing at the Llandudno site are sourced from farms across the coffee growing belt, with exclusive micro lots from Honduras, Colombia and Peru, plus a particularly special natural from Los Nogales in El Salvador.

'PUBLIC TASTING AND TRAINING EVENTS ARE ALSO IN THE PIPELINE'

You'll find Heartland beans at coffee shops throughout North Wales and beyond, though we'd recommend dropping by the new gaff for an invigorating nitro cold brew and a natter with the enthusiastic crew. Public tasting and training events are also in the pipeline – watch this space.

ESTABLISHED
2012

ROASTER
MAKE & SIZE
Coffee-Tech
Ghibli 45kg
Coffee-Tech
Ghibli 15kg
Coffee-Tech
Solar 2kg

OPEN
BY APPOINTMENT

COFFEE COURSES

BEANS AVAILABLE

ONSITE

---

www.heartlandcoffi.co.uk   T: 01492 878757

f @heartlandcoffi   🐦 @heartlandcoffi   📷 @heartlandcoffi

MAP 51. POBLADO COFFI

Unit 1, Y Barics, Nantlle, Caernarfon, Gwynedd, LL54 6BD

With Snowdonia's breathtaking peaks practically tumbling to his door, Steffan Huws must be roasting with one of the best backdrops in the UK.

While the proud Welshman currently bronzes a selection of ethically sourced beans at a former quarryman's barracks in the heart of the National Park, the Poblado story started in 2003 in Colombia where Steffan spent time learning about coffee from local farms.

On his return to Wales, he started roasting in his garden shed with a commitment to sourcing quality greens and forging sustainable partnerships.

'STEFFAN HUWS MUST BE ROASTING WITH ONE OF THE BEST BACKDROPS IN THE UK'

A trip to Rwanda reinforced his passion for transparency in the coffee chain. He says: *'There's no "one-size-fits-all" answer to ensuring we all have access to the best ethically sourced coffee, but building sustainable partnerships with producers is definitely key.'*

Poblado roasts beans from countries across the coffee growing belt and offers bespoke blends as well as a specialist selection of single origins to restaurants, cafes and farm shops across North Wales and northern England.

ESTABLISHED
2013

ROASTER
MAKE & SIZE
Giesen 15kg

OPEN
TO THE PUBLIC

COFFEE
COURSES

CUPPING
EVENTS

BEANS
AVAILABLE
ONLINE ONSITE

www.pobladocoffi.co.uk   T: 01286 882555

f @pobladocoffi   🐦 @pobladocoffi   📷 @poblado_coffi

MAP 52   TRAINING

CAFFÈ & CO.

8 Dane Court, Rainhill, Prescot, Merseyside, L35 4LU

Barista training centres often double as a cafe but few also moonlight as a creperie and ice cream parlour. Catering for every kind of espresso enthusiast, this jack of all trades offers SCA-accredited courses including Introduction to Coffee, Barista Skills, Brewing, Sensory and Latte Art, as well as How to Open a Coffee Shop.

ESTABLISHED 2011

Owner, holder of the SCA Coffee Diploma, Authorised SCA Trainer and self-professed coffee geek Neil Osthoff stocks his lab with the latest equipment and tools to ensure up-to-date training for the burgeoning baristas and home enthusiasts who hone their craft at Caffè & Co.

Neil ensures class sizes are kept small so students receive a personalised experience. He says, *'The lab is split for practical and theory. We only train up to four people as a maximum on each course.'*

And after all that hard work you can treat yourself to sweet rewards in the form of ice cream, cakes and crepes at the adjoining cafe.

www.caffeandco.com   01514 932332

@Caffè & Co.   @caffeandco   @caffe_and_co

Nº60
FOUNDATION COFFEE HOUSE - NQ

Locations are approximate

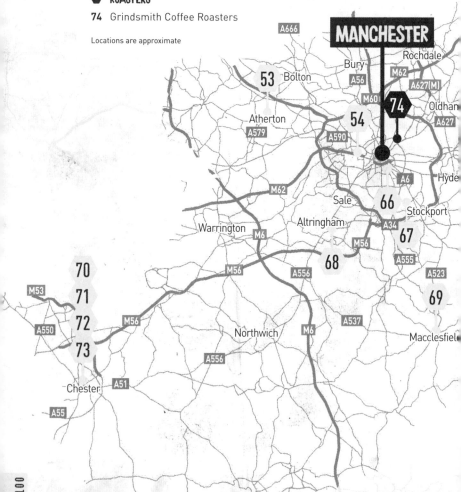

55 Pot Kettle Black
56 Atkinsons The Mackie Mayor
57 Federal Cafe & Bar
58 Just Between Friends
59 Fig + Sparrow
60 Foundation Coffee House - NQ
61 Ezra & Gil Coffee and Provisions
62 Takk Coffee House
63 Grindsmith - Deansgate
64 Foundation Coffee House - Whitworth Locke
65 Takk Espresso Bar

Locations are approximate

THE SNUG COFFEE HOUSE

67a Market Street, Atherton, Manchester, M46 0DA

Combining music, art and a healthy dose of caffeine-induced euphoria, this Atherton indie is a treasure trove of artwork-bedecked walls, colourful wooden chairs and quirky teapots.

A haven for creatives – and those simply seeking a social spot that serves a darn good brew – The Snug's cheerful vibes and chocka events list offer something for all.

Coffee geek? Drop in for a Joe Black cappuccino or guest single origin on espresso, filter or cafetiere. After a brew of a different kind? There's a top range of loose-leaf teas to tempt any pekoe pro.

PICK UP LUSH LOCAL HONEY, JAM AND CHUTNEY – SNUG STOCKS 'EM ALL

Local art lovers can potter along to The Snug's monthly late-night (and fully licensed) unplugged evenings or regular events such as Stitch 'n' Bitch (for sew pros and beginners), Atherton Hookers (for the crochet crew) and Yin Before Gin (for yoga bods and juniper junkies).

If you're stopping by for lunch, the gluten-free goodies and vegan fodder on offer are best scoffed outdoors in the suntrap courtyard off Market Street.

ESTABLISHED
2015

KEY ROASTER
Joe Black Coffee

BREWING METHODS
Espresso, filter, Chemex, cafetiere

MACHINE
Iberital

GRINDER
Iberital

OPENING HOURS
Mon-Thu
8am-4pm
Fri-Sat
8am-10pm
Sun 10am-4pm

www.thesnugatherton.com   01942 875430

f @thesnugatherton   @snugatherton   @thesnugatherton

MAP **54**

GRINDSMITH – MEDIA CITY

Unit 5-6, The Garage, Media City UK, Salford, Greater Manchester, M50 2EQ

This year, Grindsmith is not only fuelling the creative folk of Media City with top-notch coffee paired with hot-smoked mackerel power bowls – it's also revved up its own activity.

Opening a coffee development lab and roastery (with a new super clean, eco-friendly Loring Smart Roast) has given the team the opportunity to further flex their innovative muscles by creating their own branded coffee. They're even heading out to origin to buy beans at source.

PICK UP COFFEE AND MERCH AT THE RETAIL SHOP

At the cafe, the local workforce can take a break from broadcasting or enjoy some downtime from design and head to the vibrant space with its fabulous stained glass window to pair a Kalita or Chemex pourover, AeroPress or espresso with one of the wholesome brunch plates.

Especially recommended is the vegan breakfast of hash brown, spinach, mushroom, tomato, baked beans, smashed avocado, beetroot hummus and toasted rye.

ESTABLISHED
2016

HEAD ROASTER
Grindsmith
Coffee Roasters

BREWING METHOD
Kalita Wave,
Chemex,
AeroPress

MACHINE
Victoria Arduino
Black Eagle
Gravitech

GRINDER
Mythos,
Mahlkonig EK43

OPENING HOURS
Mon-Fri
7.30am-6pm
Sat 9am-6pm
Sun 9am-5pm

 Gluten FREE

 BEANS AVAILABLE — INSTORE

 ALTERNATIVE MILK

 WIFI

 OUTDOOR SEATING

 DISABLED ACCESS

 BRING YOUR OWN Cup.

www.grindsmith.com   01614 084699
@grindsmith   @grindsmiths   @grindsmithcoffee

№ 55. POT KETTLE BLACK

Barton Arcade, Deansgate, Manchester, M3 2BW

Baristas at this popular antipodean-style brunch spot in Manchester's Barton Arcade champion awesome coffee for all.

Shoppers in need of pick-me-ups, socialites meeting friends, laptop lingerers catching up on emails and budding home brewers all find a friendly welcome and an exceptional brew.

TIP BOOK THE BOARDROOM FOR A BRAINSTORM OR AN INTIMATE SOIREE

From piccolo to wilson (espresso over coconut water), there are plenty of serve styles to try from a coffee menu that makes the most of Workshop-roasted beans.

A vibrant, healthy (okay, there are a few naughty treats like the swoonsome millionaire's shortbread) and internationally inspired brekkie and lunch line-up gets credit for being thoughtfully sourced and made in house. And PKB's own bakehouse is responsible for the irresistible aroma of sourdough, pastries, cakes and brownies wafting through the industrial-inspired space.

This is also the perfect spot for post-work drinks or a tipsy weekend brunch – the cocktail, wine and beer menu is definitely worth exploring.

ESTABLISHED
2014

KEY ROASTER
Workshop Coffee

BREWING METHOD
Espresso, V60, AeroPress, batch brew

MACHINE
La Marzocco Linea PB

GRINDER
Mahlkonig EK43

OPENING HOURS
Mon-Sat
8am-7pm
Sun 9am-5pm

Gluten FREE

BEANS AVAILABLE INSTORE

ALTERNATIVE MILK

WIFI

CYCLE FRIENDLY

OUTDOOR SEATING

FAMILY FRIENDLY

DISABLED ACCESS

BRING YOUR OWN CUP

COFFEE COURSES

www.potkettleblackltd.co.uk
f @pkbcoffee   @pkbcoffee   @pkbcoffee

MAP 56 | MANCHESTER

ATKINSONS THE MACKIE MAYOR

1 Eagle Street, Manchester, M4 5BU

Pulling shots on a stunning Sanremo Opera until 11pm on weekends, the crew at Atkinsons are bringing quality caffeine – and speciality grade cocktails – to Manchester's late night revellers.

Every cortado, Kalita and cold brew served at their first residence outside of Lancaster is roasted in store. Visitors to the magnificently reimagined meat market can watch roaster Will bronze the next batch of beans on a beautifully restored vintage Uno which was only saved from extinction by 3D engineering its missing parts.

On-tap nitro is new to the bold blue and white bar this year, with silky smooth house-roasted cold brew reviving weary shoppers and caffeine tourists when the temperature soars.

TIP LEARN TO SIP 'N' SLURP LIKE A PRO AT THE FREE SUNDAY LUNCHTIME CUPPING SESSION

The Grade II-listed building is stuffed full of indie restaurants and artisan street food. Ease in with a flat white at Atkinsons then take your pick of the food hall's smorgasbord of bao buns, stone-baked pizzas and rotisserie chicken before going full-circle and finishing with a spiced rooibos tea negroni nightcap at the cafe.

ESTABLISHED
2017

KEY ROASTER
Atkinsons Coffee Roasters

BREWING METHOD
Espresso, Marco SP9, Kalita Wave

MACHINE
Sanremo Opera

GRINDER
Mythos One Clima Pro, Mahlkonig EK43

OPENING HOURS
Tue-Thu 8am-10pm
Fri 8am-11pm
Sat 9am-11pm
Sun 9am-8pm

FEDERAL CAFE & BAR

MAP No 57

9 Nicholas Croft, Manchester, M4 1EY

Ask the clan of antipodean expats where they go for a morning flattie in Manchester and there's a good chance they'll say Federal.

Like any good Down Under drinking den, this place specialises in top-notch speciality coffee (with or without booze), all-day eggs and laid-back vibes.

Brunch is an all-Aussie affair, with the likes of halloumi and 'shrooms, corn fritters, french toast and smashed avo served with a cheery *'g'day'*.

TIP
TRY THE HOUSE-MADE SUPERMAN JUICE FOR A FRUIT-AND-VEG-TASTIC BOOST

Collaborations with fellow small businesses have provided fresh inspo for the Federal fraternity this year: local beers from Cloudwater and Runaway breweries fuel post-work drinks, a new floral installation from Frog Flowers has freshened up the cafe space and local artwork adds community spirit.

London's Ozone provides NZ-inspired blends and single origins – sip 'em in store then stock up on retail bags so you can recreate the magic at home.

ESTABLISHED
2014

KEY ROASTER
Ozone Coffee Roasters

BREWING METHODS
Espresso, V60, AeroPress, cold brew

MACHINE
La Marzocco Linea PB

GRINDER
Mahlkonig EK43, Victoria Arduino Mythos One

OPENING HOURS
Mon-Fri
7.30am-6pm
Sat 8am-6pm
Sun 8am-5pm

Gluten FREE

BEANS AVAILABLE INSTORE

ALTERNATIVE MILK

WIFI

OUTDOOR SEATING

FAMILY FRIENDLY

BRING YOUR OWN CUP

www.federalcafe.co.uk   01618 319374

federalcafebar   federalcafebar   federalcafebar

JUST BETWEEN FRIENDS

56 Tib Street, Manchester, M4 1LG

L ocals tried to keep this Northern Quarter newbie to themselves when it opened on Tib Street in early 2018, but the fact that it's already thrumming with colleagues chatting caffeine and chums scoffing cake suggests that someone let slip.

To be fair to its fanbase, the capsule cafe hasn't exactly gone incognito. The word "coffee" in large letters above the bifold window, cup-adorned street sign and sandwich board signalling "espresso this way" more than hint at the space's new guise.

MAKE A RETURN TRIP FOR THE NEW SEASON BEANS FROM ASSEMBLY

With just six months under their belt, the Just Between Friends team are focusing on cracking the seasonal coffee offering. Beans from London's Assembly stump up the good stuff via the La Marzocco machine, batch brewer and pourover filters.

If you catch the cafe between the crowds, take a moment to appreciate the contemporary minimalism of the place. Hexagonal tables, leather-studded stools and a small curation of house plants all contribute to its modern vibe.

ESTABLISHED
2018

KEY ROASTER
Assembly Coffee

BREWING METHODS
Espresso,
batch brew, V60

MACHINE
La Marzocco
Linea PB

GRINDER
Victoria Arduino
Mythos One

OPENING HOURS
Mon-Fri
7.30am-4pm
Sat-Sun
8.30am-4pm

 Gluten FREE

 BEANS AVAILABLE INSTORE

 ALTERNATIVE MILK

WIFI

 OUTDOOR seating

BRING YOUR OWN Cup

www.justbetweenfriendscoffee.com

@Just Between Friends   @justbetweenfri2   @justbetweenfriendscoffee

59. FIG + SPARROW

20 Oldham Street, Northern Quarter, Manchester, M1 1JN

If you're going to serve incredible coffee in a beautifully designed setting, it's only right to enable customers to pick up a few pieces in store to fashion their own slice of cafe culture at home.

Happily, Fig & Sparrow's design-shop-meets-brunch-stop provides a constant stream of interior inspiration for the latte lovers and creatives who flock to its Northern Quarter nest.

Rosetta-flourished flatties, colourful lunch bowls and chunky slabs of millionaire's shortbread turn out to be as delicious as they are aesthetically pleasing. Take the time to browse the boards of brunch and lunch staples while the baristas craft the latest seasonal single origin on filter.

TIP CAFFEINE OVERKILL? TRY THE BLENDSMITHS BEETROOT LATTE

Sandwiches (such as the pesto, mozzarella and sundried tomato number) and salad sides feature stonking bread from the team at Trove. If you visit early, you can even nab a loaf to add to your haul of greeting cards, books and coffee soap to take home.

ESTABLISHED
2013

KEY ROASTER
Climpson
& Sons

BREWING METHOD
Espresso,
AeroPress, V60,
Chemex

MACHINE
La Marzocco
Linea PB

GRINDER
Victoria Arduino
Mythos One,
Mahlkonig EK43

OPENING HOURS
Mon-Fri
8am-7pm
Sat 9am-7pm
Sun 10am-7pm

www.figandsparrow.co.uk | 07815 137563

@figsparrow @figsparrow @figsparrow

MAP 60.

FOUNDATION COFFEE HOUSE – NQ

Sevendale House, Lever Street, Manchester, M1 1JB

Fed up of sinking the same old morning flattie? You need a trip to Foundation.

These guys specialise in a unique line-up of quirky caffeinations: try the red eye, black eye or dead eye (filter coffee with one, two or [gulp] three shots of espresso). Or set your sights on a bulletproof (black coffee with butter and coconut oil) for silky smooth sipping.

If the sun's past the yard arm, an espresso martini is a good call for its foamy blend of espresso, Mr Black Cold Brew Coffee Liqueur, Black Cow pure milk vodka and brown sugar.

You can even polish up your mixology skills at one of the house cocktail masterclasses (barista courses and tea experiences also feature).

TIP COFFEED OUT? HIT UP THE SPECIALITY HOT CHOCS FROM AROUND THE GLOBE

Other reasons to visit include yoga sessions, movie nights and, of course, the brunch menu: the french toast changes each week while seductive vegan vibes come in the form of canellini beans with garlic, rosemary, thyme and lemon on toast.

ESTABLISHED
2015

KEY ROASTER
Origin Coffee Roasters

BREWING METHODS
Espresso, Kalita Wave, V60, AeroPress, Chemex

MACHINE
La Marzocco Linea PB

GRINDER
Mythos One x 2, Mahlkonig EK43

OPENING HOURS
Mon-Tue
7.30am-7pm
Wed-Fri
7.30am-10pm
Sat 9am-10pm
Sun 9am-7pm

www.foundationcoffeehouse.co.uk | 01612 388633

@fdncoffee @fdncoffee @fdncoffee

ATKINSONS

COFFEE ROASTERS

www.thecoffeehopper.com
f : facebook.com/atkinsonscoffee
i : @atkinsons.coffee
t : @coffeehopper

EZRA & GIL COFFEE AND PROVISIONS

20 Hilton Street, Northern Quarter, Manchester, M1 1FR

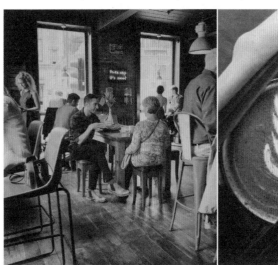

With Ezra translating to 'helper' and Gil meaning 'happiness', this Northern Quarter cafe is perking up its customers' days – one flat white and caramel slice at a time.

Pass the urban cafe and let the scent of freshly ground ManCoCo beans and the intoxicating hum of activity pull you in to where the baristas work their magic on the La Marzocco machine and small collection of filter kit.

PLENTY OF PUSHCHAIR SPACE MAKES THIS ONE FOR THE WHOLE FAMILY

Customer service tops the agenda for manager Lizzie Harper, and her whole team work hard to make their customers feel at home in the industrial-chic space. Braille menus are available on request, and the chatty rabble behind the busy bar are always up for recommending their current faves from the brunch specials.

The perfect spot to gather with friends for brunch, expect a prolonged period of silence while your party contemplates the various options including house-baked granola, french toast and smashed pumpkin.

ESTABLISHED
2015

ManCoCo

Espresso, V60, french press

La Marzocco Linea PB

Fiorenzato F83

Mon-Fri
7.30am-8pm
Sat-Sun
8am-7pm

WIFI

www.ezraandgil.com

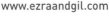
@ezraandgil   @ezra_gil   @ezraandgil

TAKK COFFEE HOUSE

6 Tarriff Street, Northern Quarter, Manchester, M1 2FF

A bazaar of beans awaits at this Nordic-inspired hangout in Manchester's Northern Quarter.

Alongside the house roast from Clifton, Takk's weekly curation spans from Berlin's well-established The Barn to Copenhagen's inspirational Coffee Collective to Wiltshire's all-women roastery, Girls Who Grind. And owner Philip Hannaway is keen to top last year's achievement of serving beans from 25 roasteries.

'Sure, it would be easier to stick to one roaster but the diversity and personality is what made us fall in love with speciality coffee, and we love to share this with everyone,' he says.

LOOK OUT FOR TAKK'S NEW MANCHESTER UNI VENTURE – LAUNCHING SOON

'Coffee is in our DNA so everything is done with love and respect for the product.'

This passion for perfection includes fuelling coffee fiends with a simple but delicious all-day brunch menu. Try the 'nduja and eggs (spicy sausage, poached egg, avo and luscious salsa verde on Manchester-baked sourdough) for a fiery start to the day – and ask the knowledgeable baristas for the perfect brew to accompany it.

ESTABLISHED
2013

KEY ROASTER
Clifton Coffee Roasters

BREWING METHOD
Espresso, V60, Chemex, AeroPress, batch brew

MACHINE
La Marzocco Linea PB

GRINDER
Mahlkonig K30, Mahlkonig EK43, Mythos One Clima Pro

OPENING HOURS
Mon-Fri 8am-6pm
Sat 9am-5pm
Sun 10am-5pm

 Gluten FREE

 BEANS AVAILABLE INSTORE

 ALTERNATIVE MILK

 WIFI

 CYCLE FRIENDLY

 OUTDOOR SEATING

 FAMILY FRIENDLY

 BRING YOUR OWN CUP

www.takkmcr.com

 @takkmcr @takkmcr @takkmcr

GRINDSMITH – DEANSGATE

MAP: 63.

231-233 Deansgate, Manchester, M3 4EN

Everyone wants to work at Grindsmith. But you don't need to be a barista looking to pull shots through the Black Eagle or be lusting after the job of adding the final toasty touch to a grilled bagel, as the cafe is also Manchester's freelancer HQ.

Join the horde commuting to Grindsmith each day, set up your laptop at one of the many co-working spots and grab an AeroPress for a morning of super productivity.

SWITCH UP YOUR REGULAR COFFEE FOR A NITRO COLD BREW IN SUMMER

At 3,650 square feet in size, Grindsmith is the city's largest coffee shop and always abuzz with creativity and caffeine.

The team behind the slick set-up have recently started roasting on an eco Loring Smart Roast at their development lab in Ancoats, so the flat whites have never been finer.

As the morning draws to a close, move on to the range of well-stuffed sarnies and, come mid-afternoon, the sweet stuff. You can't do genius work with low blood sugar levels, right?

ESTABLISHED
2014

KEY ROASTER
Grindsmith
Coffee Roasters

BREWING METHOD
Espresso,
Kalita Wave,
Chemex,
AeroPress

MACHINE
Victoria Arduino
Black Eagle
Gravitech

GRINDER
Mythos,
Mahlkonig EK43

OPENING HOURS
Mon-Fri
8am-8pm
Sat 8am-6pm
Sun 9am-5pm

 Gluten FREE

 BEANS AVAILABLE INSTORE

 ALTERNATIVE MILK

 WIFI

OUTDOOR seating

 DISABLED ACCESS

 BRING YOUR OWN cup

www.grindsmith.com   07496 798220

@grindsmith   @grindsmiths   @grindsmithcoffee

MAP 64. FOUNDATION COFFEE HOUSE – WHITWORTH LOCKE

74 Princess Street, Manchester, M1 6JD

The second Foundation outpost will open its doors in November 2018 and promises more of the glorious caffeine kicks it's already famed for on Lever Street.

Located in the beautiful new Locke Hotel, the contemporary decor (a mature reimagining of the original shop's slick set-up) provides seriously stylish surroundings for your morning pick-me-up or late night espresso martini.

TIP EARLY BIRDS, SWING BY FIRST THING WHEN BATCH BREW IS JUST £1 A CUP

As with its sister cafe, this new spot will feature a moreishly good menu – of both the food and coffee variety.

Serving Origin beans via a medley of different methods – espresso, V60, AeroPress and Kalita Wave – along with more unusual finds such as bulletproof and kevlar, this is a find for adventurous coffee fiends.

Events, monthly exhibitions and coffee courses are added attractions and there's also a co-working space in the lobby, so whether your visit is for work or play, Foundation's a great stop at any time.

ESTABLISHED
2018

KEY ROASTER
Origin Coffee Roasters

BREWING METHOD
Espresso, V60, AeroPress, Kalita Wave

MACHINE
La Marzocco Linea PB ABR

GRINDER
Mythos One, Mahlkonig EK43

OPENING HOURS
Mon-Sun
7.30am-11pm

www.foundationcoffeehouse.co.uk   07507 318043

@fdncoffee   @fdncoffee   @fdncoffee

TAKK ESPRESSO BAR

MAP

Unit 1, Hatch, Oxford Road, Manchester, M1 7ED

Ask the caffeine cognoscenti where to get a killer coffee in the heart of Manchester's city centre and you may well be directed to two repurposed shipping containers tucked away amid the bustle of Oxford Road.

An urban oasis of caffeinated pleasure, Takk's Espresso Bar offers brilliant coffee served with Nordic flair and friendliness.

The popular house roast of Finca Miravalle from El Salvador is always a good shout, although adventurous imbibers may want to plump for the second espresso option which showcases seasonal beans from a well-curated portfolio of roasteries.

KEEP AN EYE ON SOCIAL MEDIA FOR NEWS OF TAKEOVERS, TALKS AND TASTINGS

Office folk work a fast fix into their schedule at this coffee shop which sits within Hatch (the city's quirky retail, food and drink destination), while lazy lunchers and laptop tappers like to linger in the large outdoor seating area or airy indoor spaces.

Reached peak caffeine? Pop next door to sister brewery, ÖL Nano, for a cool selection of craft beers.

ESTABLISHED
2017

ROASTER
Clifton Coffee Roasters

BREWING METHODS
Espresso, batch brew

MACHINE
La Marzocco Linea PB

GRINDER
Mythos One Clima Pro, Mahlkonig EK43

OPENING HOURS
Mon-Fri
8am-6pm
Sat 9am-6pm
Sun 10am-5pm

www.takkmcr.com

@takkmcr   @takkmcr   @takkmcr

66. THE ANCHOR COFFEE HOUSE

508 Moss Lane East, Manchester, M14 4PA

The Monmouth coffee isn't the only thing fuelling the feel-good factor at this volunteer-powered coffee shop, as leaving a suspended coffee for someone in need also provides a buzz.

Bolstering the feel good vibes at this unusual speciality-driven project is the small band of baristas who spend their days pouring V60s and pulling espresso behind the bar.

They're managed by Steph and Amy who do a sterling job of training up the existing and new recruits on the monthly selection of single origins stocking the second Mazzer grinder. The friendly bunch are always searching for new members if you're looking to sharpen your espresso skills.

TIP: THE NEW SUMMER AFFOGATO SERVE IS MELTINGLY GOOD

Make your visit one-of-a-kind and pair the latest guest bean (past residencies have included 3FE, Dark Woods and Olfactory) with the bagel of the month, then grab a spot in the roomy outdoor seating area.

Maxed out on coffee? Try one of the Manchester-made, small-batch sodas and a slice of something sweet sourced from one of a clutch of local indie bakeries.

ESTABLISHED
2013

KEY ROASTER
Monmouth
Coffee Company

BREWING METHOD
Espresso, V60

MACHINE
La Marzocco
GB5

GRINDER
Mythos One
Clima Pro,
Mazzer x 2

OPENING HOURS
Mon-Fri
9am-5pm
Sat 10am-4pm

www.anchorcoffee.co.uk   01612 488772

f @anchorcoffeehouse   @anchorcoffee   @anchorcoffee

NOOK

111 Heaton Moor Road, Heaton Moor, Stockport, Cheshire, SK4 4HY

Doors on the ceiling, tiles on the stairs and hilariously quirky notes scribbled on the blackboard outside: there's an *Alice In Wonderland*-style surrealism to this popular cafe and bottle shop in the heart of Heaton Moor.

As the name suggests, Nook is a cosy space where you can enjoy a touch of whimsy with your flat white or a dash of eccentricity with your espresso.

TIP DON'T MISS THE BRILLIANT OPEN MIC NIGHT EACH THURSDAY

Manchester's Passion Fruit and Leeds' North Star provide consistently great beans, while a roster of guest roasters such as Heart and Graft and ManCoCo add adventurous alternatives.

And should you find your caffeine limit coming close to capacity there are plenty of other potable potions on the menu – including craft beer, gin and wine.

At lunch and brekkie the team set out to make the most of local ingredients in sterling soups, stews, sandwiches and wraps, complemented by a wicked selection of homemade cakes and bakes.

ESTABLISHED
2014

KEY ROASTER
Multiple roasters

BREWING METHOD
Espresso, AeroPress, Chemex, V60, batch filter, french press

MACHINE
La Marzocco Linea PB

GRINDER
Mazzer Mini

OPENING HOURS
Mon-Wed
8.30am-9.30pm
Thu-Fri
8.30am-11pm
Sat 9am-11pm
Sun 9.30am-9.30pm

 Gluten FREE

 BEANS AVAILABLE INSTORE

 ALTERNATIVE MILK

 WIFI

 CYCLE FRIENDLY

 OUTDOOR SEATING

 FAMILY FRIENDLY

 BRING YOUR OWN Cup

www.nooknc.co.uk   01614 325385

@thenooknc   @thenooknc   @thenooknc

MAP№ 68. TWO BROTHERS COFFEE

53 Stamford New Road, Altrincham, Cheshire, WA14 1DS

The realms of quality coffee and electrical engineering rarely cross wires, yet brothers Dave and Steve have successfully fused their two passions at Altrincham's latest speciality player.

While the cafe's blueprint-inspired machine mural, bookcase brimming with engineering books and industrial-style lighting hint at the duo's day jobs, the haul of speciality brew gear and collection of beans suggest incredible caffeine is more than a pastime.

TIP LOOK OUT FOR CUPPINGS WITH LOCAL ROASTERS SUCH AS ATKINSONS

With two espressos and four filter coffees to sample at any time, there's always something new and noteworthy to be discovered here. Lancaster roaster Atkinsons and Manchester's Ancoats hold regular residencies on the Sanremo machine, while other guests make shorter appearances on filter.

If you're deciding between cold drip and nitro or washed and natural, and you haven't had a lightbulb moment, the clued-up baristas are full of suggestions.

'We'll happily chat about the coffee for days if that's your thing,' says manager Sean. *'If not, we're not precious. We'll let you come to your own conclusions.'*

ESTABLISHED
2017

KEY ROASTER
Atkinsons Coffee Roasters

BREWING METHODS
Espresso, V60, syphon, batch brew, drip, nitro

MACHINE
Sanremo Opera

GRINDER
Mythos One Clima Pro, Mahlkonig EK43

OPENING HOURS
Mon-Fri 7am-5pm
Sat 8am-5pm
Sun 9.30am-4pm

Gluten FREE

BEANS AVAILABLE INSTORE

ALTERNATIVE MILK

WIFI

CYCLE FRIENDLY

OUTDOOR SEATING

FAMILY FRIENDLY

DISABLED ACCESS

BRING YOUR OWN Cup

COFFEE COURSES

www.twobrothers.coffee   01616 131821

 @twobrotherscoffeeltd   @twobrothers_alt   @twobrotherscoffee

FLOUR WATER SALT

9 Market Place, Macclesfield, Cheshire, SK10 1EB

Flour Water Salt champions real bread via a roll call of daily baked rye breads, ciabatta, baguettes and more.

What started in 2009 with sourdough soon expanded to pastry, and the talented team of bakers and pastry chefs now fashion some of the finest croissants, sugar buns and fruit-laden danish this side of the country.

FIND THE FWS VAN AT THE TREACLE MARKET ON THE LAST SUNDAY OF EACH MONTH

Moving to a roomier spot on Market Place in 2018 (and honouring the three simple ingredients forming each loaf in bold letters above the door), owner Paul saw the opportunity not only to bring his beautiful bakes to the masses but also to improve Macc's speciality coffee offering.

Visitors in search of their daily bread can now enjoy a carefully poured ManCoCo espresso alongside their pick of the weekly changing brunch and lunch menu and a counter crowded with freshly lacquered pastries.

'We're a bakery at heart,' says Paul, *'though we want the quality of the coffee to meet that of the food.'*

ESTABLISHED
2017

1ST CHOICE
ManCoCo

BREWING METHOD
Espresso

MACHINE
La Marzocco
Linea Classic

GRINDER
Mazzer Robur

OPENING HOURS
Tue-Sat
8.30am-2.30pm

MILK

WIFI

www.flourwatersalt.co.uk   07714 419646

@flourwatersaltuk   @_flourwatersalt   @_flourwatersalt

70. SHORT + STOUT

3a Ermine Road, Hoole, Chester, Cheshire, CH2 3PN

Chester's coffee scene has enjoyed a growth spurt this year and seen the likes of Short + Stout join its burgeoning list of speciality players.

Eight years of cafe hopping in Melbourne inspired owners Sarah and Will Noden to introduce a slice of Aussie cafe culture to their Hoole neighbourhood – so expect chilled vibes, all-day brunch and lip-smackingly good coffee.

Short + Stout's tall windows and white and bleached wood palette make for a light-filled spot where you can grab a bar stool or seat at one of the compact tables and linger over an Ancoats espresso.

FEELING THE HEAT? TRY AN ICED COCONUT MATCHA LATTE

Guest roasters such as Hundred House and Heartland feature as cold brew in summer and batch brew in colder months.

In addition to quality coffee, brunch heroes such as the avocado toast and poached eggs on sourdough are quickly bolstering Short + Stout's stature in Chester's foodie rankings.

ESTABLISHED
2018

KEY ROASTER
Ancoats Coffee Co.

BREWING METHOD
Espresso,
cold brew,
batch brew

MACHINE
La Marzocco
Linea PB

GRINDER
Mythos One
Clima Pro,
Mazzer Mini

OPENING HOURS
Mon-Fri
7.30am-5pm
Sat 8am-4pm
Sun 9.30am-2pm

Gluten FREE

BEANS AVAILABLE
INSTORE

ALTERNATIVE MILK

WIFI

FAMILY FRIENDLY

BRING YOUR OWN cup

01244 343378

@SHORT + STOUT @shortandstout_ @shortandstoutltd

MAP 71. LITTLE YELLOW PIG

31 Westminster Road, Hoole, Chester, Cheshire, CH2 3AX

Having met in a cafe in Hoole and bonding over a mutual interest in speciality, it was only fitting that Richard and Lucy's relationship would lead them on a shared journey into quality coffee.

Taking the plunge in 2014 and leasing a cosy corner building in the suburb, the pair used their shared passions – skateboards, vinyl and Lego – to make Chester's Little Yellow Pig a pleasingly unique find.

The local following of espresso lovers and cake addicts has led this little piggy to Best Cafe glory (as a three-time finalist) at the Cheshire Food and Drink Awards, and at weekends you'll find fans gleefully chowing down on homemade brunch dishes, digging into epic slices of flapjack and sipping perfectly poured flat whites.

TIP: LUCY'S MUM BAKES BANGING CAKES, INCLUDING AN INCREDIBLE ELDERFLOWER AND LEMON NUMBER

Caffeinated alchemy comes courtesy of London's Dark Arts, with a nifty new drip filter set-up luring Hoole's black-coffee dodgers to the dark side. Don't fret if you're not feeling experimental – the chilled-out team will still craft you something magic on the La Marzocco.

ESTABLISHED
2014

KEY ROASTER
Dark Arts Coffee

BREWING METHOD
Espresso,
cold brew,
batch filter

MACHINE
La Marzocco
Linea Classic

GRINDER
Mythos One
Clima Pro

OPENING HOURS
Mon-Fri
9am-5pm
Sat 9am-4pm
Sun 10am-2pm

Gluten FREE

BEANS AVAILABLE INSTORE

ALTERNATIVE MILK

WIFI

CYCLE FRIENDLY

FAMILY FRIENDLY

01244 637220

@littleyellowpighoole   @littleyellowpig   @littleyellowpig31

THE FLOWER CUP

61 Watergate Row South, Chester, Cheshire, CH1 2LE

Guaranteed to earn a lot of love on the 'gram, a slick set-up combining kickass coffee, dreamy all-day brunch dishes and an in-house flower shop mean the only filter you'll need at this picture-worthy spot comes courtesy of the Clever Dripper.

Working with single origin lovelies from Liverpool's Neighbourhood Coffee, the posy of knowledgeable baristas are as committed to crafting excellent espresso based brews as they are to tending the plants and flowers that fill this urban jungle.

Last year's kitchen upgrade has allowed the team to further grow The Flower Cup's offer. Think classic brunch fare with offbeat options such as brekkie tacos stuffed with egg, halloumi, avocado and sriracha, along with a healthy selection of vegan dishes including shakshuka, sweet potato hash and plump chocolate pancakes.

GOT GREEN FINGERS? HONE YOUR SKILLS AT THE IN-HOUSE FLORISTRY CLASSES

Next season, owner Milli Ball plans to introduce more seating (and a new florist shop next door) which will provide intrepid Instagrammers with even more room and inspiration for their #latteart pics.

ESTABLISHED
2016

KEY ROASTER
Neighbourhood Coffee

BREWING METHODS
Espresso,
Clever Dripper

MACHINE
La Spaziale S5
EKTA

GRINDER
Mahlkonig On Demand

OPENING HOURS
Mon-Sat
9am-5pm
Sun 10am-5pm

www.flowercup.co.uk   01244 639634

@flowercupchester   @theflowercupch1   @theflowercupchester

MAP 73.

JAUNTY GOAT COFFEE

57 Bridge Street, Chester, Cheshire, CH1 1NG

You know a coffee shop is doing something right when it's still spilling over with people post-4pm on a sunny summer's day.

Whether it's the result of the house-roasted beans filling the hopper, the simple plates of gorgeous grub or the copper-plated, clean-lined and irresistibly Instagrammable interior, you'll rarely find more than a couple of tables for the taking at Jaunty Goat.

THE STONKING CARROT CAKE IS AN ABSOLUTE GAME-CHANGER

Window bar seating and communal tables throng with foodies grazing on tropical fruit bowls, smoked haddock kedgeree and shiitake mushrooms from the seasonal menu, as well as coffee folk sipping nitro cold brew and adding beautifully crafted flatties to their camera roll.

A second Mazzer hosts a monthly guest coffee from a regional roaster such as Ancoats, North Star or ManCoCo. And fans of the new Jaunty Goat house roast can stock up from the retail selection which also includes a small curation of filter gear.

ESTABLISHED
2015

KEY ROASTER
Jaunty Goat
Coffee Company

BREWING METHODS
Espresso,
AeroPress, V60,
Chemex, nitro

MACHINE
Conti Monte
Carlo,
Sanremo Opera

GRINDER
Mazzer Robur,
Mazzer Major,
Mazzer Super
Jolly Timer

OPENING HOURS
Mon-Sun
8am-6pm

www.jauntygoatcoffee.co.uk   01244 421492

@jauntygoat   @jauntygoat_   @jauntygoat_

ROASTERS

GREATER
MANCHESTER
& CHESHIRE

74. GRINDSMITH COFFEE ROASTERS

Unit 6, Varley Business Centre, Manchester, M40 8EL

The innovation-fuelled team at Grindsmith have taken another step in their journey this year with the launch of a speciality roastery and coffee laboratory.

It follows the introduction of a coffee pod in 2014, followed by the co-working cafe space on Deansgate and then the creation of its Media City cathedral to coffee in 2016.

Based in Ancoats – the former heart of Manchester's industrial revolution – the roasting team continue to embody the city's busy-bee ethos through the baking of beans imported from all over the world.

The new hive of innovation focuses on roasting, quality control and research. Phase two will see the development of a barista training academy on site.

ESTABLISHED
2018

ROASTER
MAKE & SIZE
Loring S15 15kg
Falcon 15kg

OPEN
BY APPOINTMENT

COFFEE
COURSES

COURSES

BEANS
AVAILABLE
ONLINE ONSITE

'OUR AIM IS TO HELP MANCHESTER PUSH THE BOUNDARIES'

New kit at the slick space includes the purchase of a Loring Smart Roast, with its odourless, flavour-locking roasting system, and a coffee laboratory.

Grindsmith co-founder Pete Gibson says, *'Our aim is to become a centre of excellence and innovation within the industry, and help Manchester push the boundaries of knowledge and research within speciality coffee.'*

---

www.grindsmith.com T: 01614 084699

f @grindsmith 🐦 @grindsmiths 📷 @grindsmithcoffee

NORTH AND WEST YORKSHIRE

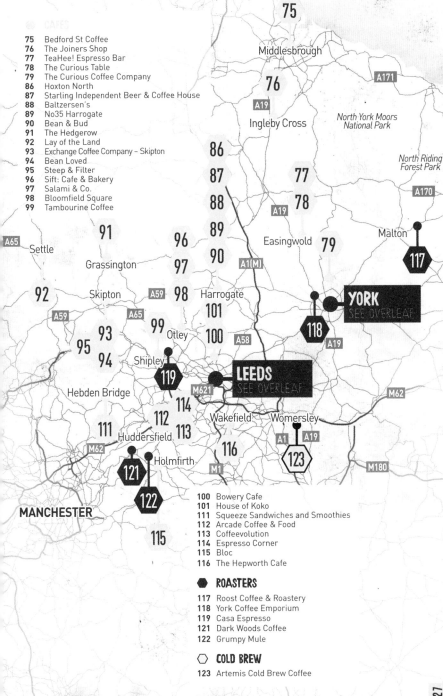

75 Bedford St Coffee
76 The Joiners Shop
77 TeaHee! Espresso Bar
78 The Curious Table
79 The Curious Coffee Company
86 Hoxton North
87 Starling Independent Beer & Coffee House
88 Baltzersen's
89 No35 Harrogate
90 Bean & Bud
91 The Hedgerow
92 Lay of the Land
93 Exchange Coffee Company – Skipton
94 Bean Loved
95 Steep & Filter
96 Sift: Cafe & Bakery
97 Salami & Co.
98 Bloomfield Square
99 Tambourine Coffee

100 Bowery Cafe
101 House of Koko
111 Squeeze Sandwiches and Smoothies
112 Arcade Coffee & Food
113 Coffeevolution
114 Espresso Corner
115 Bloc
116 The Hepworth Cafe

⬡ **ROASTERS**

117 Roost Coffee & Roastery
118 York Coffee Emporium
119 Casa Espresso
121 Dark Woods Coffee
122 Grumpy Mule

⬡ **COLD BREW**

123 Artemis Cold Brew Coffee

LEEDS

DURHAM

DEANGATE
GOODRAMGATE
ALDWARK
80
81
82
BLAKE ST
STONEGATE
LOW PETERGATE
COLLIERGATE
83 124
LENDAL
ST. SAVIOURGATE
NEW ST
SHAMBLES
CONEY ST
FOSSGATE
85
NORTH ST
PICCADILLY
COPPERGATE
84
CASTLEG
KING ST
CASTLE
FET
FAX ST
MPDEN ST
VICTOR ST
CROMWELL R
KYM
ELDERGATE

CAFES

80 Brew & Brownie
81 Burr Coffee
82 Spring Espresso – Lendal
83 The Attic and Cafe Harlequin
84 Spring Espresso – Fossgate
85 The Fossgate Social

○ **TRAINING**

124 Northern Academy of Coffee

Locations are approximate

YORK

75. BEDFORD ST COFFEE

27 Bedford Street, Middlesbrough, North Yorkshire, TS1 2LL

The first speciality shop from the guys at Rounton Coffee Roasters, Bedford St is the antidote to the cafe chains which crowd Middlesbrough's city centre.

Set in the new food and drink quarter, it's a hideaway from the bustle of the surrounding urban streets. With its dark wood interior, hanging pendant lights and Wifi on tap, it's well suited to those who like working to the clink of cups and hiss of the steam wand while sipping the good stuff.

There's a selection of Rounton's single origin espresso to choose from – all of which are sustainably sourced – as well as a monthly guest filter featured from a rotating reel of European roasters. As for the food, fruity porridge bowls and lip-smacking smoothies tempt laptop lingerers to stick around a while longer.

CHECK OUT THE MONTHLY COFFEE TASTING SESH WITH ROUNTON ROASTERS

Every month the team take part in the Orange Pip Market – a vibrant event where indie stalls, street food vendors and local retailers gather in the quarter for festival vibes and family fun.

ESTABLISHED
2016

KEY ROASTER
Rounton Coffee Roasters

BREWING METHODS
Espresso, V60, AeroPress, cold brew

MACHINE
Sanremo Verona RS

GRINDER
Mahlkonig K30

OPENING HOURS
Mon-Fri
8am-4pm
Sat 9am-4pm

BEANS AVAILABLE INSTORE

ALTERNATIVE MILK

WIFI

DISABLED ACCESS

BRING YOUR OWN Cup

www.rountoncoffee.co.uk　01642 647856

@bedfordstcoffee　　@bedfordstcoffee　　@bedfordstcoffee

THE JOINERS SHOP

Cross Lane, Ingleby Cross, Northallerton, North Yorkshire, DL6 3ND

A killer flat white is an oasis in the desert for weary road trippers travelling north Yorkshire's winding country roads. And any speciality fans who stumble across this rural gem won't believe their luck when they see the bounty of own-roasted beans behind the bar.

It's not just the Rounton espresso and homemade cold brew that has ramblers fresh from the footpath rejoicing though, as The Joiners Shop is also setting up staycationers traversing the Wainwright's Coast to Coast path with an award winning brekkie.

KEEP BIG KIDS HAPPY WITH AN EPIC SLICE OF KINDER BUENO CAKE

Scooping the Best Breakfast in Hambleton gong just six months after opening, this village cafe is taking Northallerton's foodie offering to the next level. Weekend lunch specials such as prawn and pesto pasta and yellow chicken curry receive similar praise from the locals, and the afternoon tea is also worth the trip.

Stock up on roasted-down-the-road beans for onward travels; the retail selection of Rounton bags includes seasonal single origins and the Granary house blend.

ESTABLISHED
2017

KEY ROASTER
Rounton Coffee Roasters

BREWING METHODS
Espresso, cold brew

MACHINE
Sanremo Verona RS

GRINDER
Mahlkonig K30

OPENING HOURS
Mon-Sat
9.30am-4pm
Sun 10am-4pm

 Gluten FREE

 BEANS AVAILABLE INSTORE

 ALTERNATIVE MILK

 WIFI

 CYCLE FRIENDLY

 OUTDOOR SEATING

 FAMILY FRIENDLY

 DISABLED ACCESS

 BRING YOUR OWN Cup

www.rountoncoffee.co.uk   01609 882762

@thejoinersshop   @thejoinersshop   @thejoinersshop

TEAHEE! ESPRESSO BAR

Old Toll Booth, 3 Market Place, York, North Yorkshire, YO61 3AB

A former toll keeper's cottage is the unusual setting for this coffee shop which has proved to be a big hit for its combination of quality espresso, loose-leaf teas and award winning bakes.

Leeds' North Star stumps up the goods for the house roast while guests include Union, Vagabond and Origin, so there's always something new and noteworthy in the hopper.

Aside from coffee, Teahee! has garnered a reputation for its homemade light lunches and irresistible cakes.

TAKE A PEW IN ONE OF THE CHAPEL CHAIRS WHICH HAVE FOUND A NEW HOME AT TEAHEE!

Signature bakes include a zesty Tunisian orange cake, glorious salted caramel brownies and the ever-popular three seed flapjack.

The interior is all rustic charm, with original features paying homage to its Georgian market town setting. If you're up for coffee alfresco, there's a cluster of tables out front plus a secluded courtyard garden in which to linger with your brew – or a craft beer or glass of wine.

ESTABLISHED
2003

KEY ROASTER
North Star
Coffee Roasters

BREWING METHOD
Espresso,
french press

MACHINE
Sanremo
Verona RS

GRINDER
Mahlkonig K30,
Mazzer Mini

OPENING HOURS
Mon-Sat
8am-4pm
Sun 10am-3pm

MILK

WIFI

www.teahee.co.uk   01347 823533

@teahees   @teahee

THE CURIOUS TABLE

Market Place, Easingwold, York, North Yorkshire, YO61 3AG

'**C**ome for the brownies; stay for the quirky vibe' should be the motto at this Easingwold find. Although it's renowned for the award winning (and secret recipe) brownies served with every cup, The Curious Table has garnered a foodie following for more than its moreishly moist bite-sized squares.

Sharing platters, fruit-laden french toast and deli sandwiches tussle for visitors' attention on a seasonal menu which is stocked by a legion of local suppliers. Gluten dodgers and vegan visitors are always welcome to ask for off-piste options as everything is freshly prepared to order.

IN SUMMER, SINK INTO A COMFY BEANBAG ON THE GREEN

Named for its unique interior and individually crafted tables, the urge to stand out from the crowd also shines through in the cafe's signature coffee blend. Roasted and prepared at nearby York Coffee Emporium, it's a delectable mix of beans from Vietnam, Ethiopia, Brazil and Guatemala.

And if you visit for coffee, you won't be able to miss the towering wall of local preserves, beans and artisan goodies opposite the bar, so be sure to pack a roomy shopper for your trip.

ESTABLISHED
2013

KEY ROASTER
York Coffee Emporium

BREWING METHOD
Espresso, AeroPress, french press

MACHINE
Cimbali

GRINDER
Cimbali Magnum

OPENING HOURS
Mon-Fri 7.30am-5pm
Sat 8.30am-4pm
Sun 9.30am-3pm

www.thecurioustable.co.uk   01347 823434

@thecurioustable   @thecurioustable   @curious.table

79. THE CURIOUS COFFEE COMPANY

Unit 8, Haxby Shopping Centre, Haxby, York, North Yorkshire, YO32 2LU

Before speciality stole his heart, Curious Coffee Co founder Eddie Copley-Farnell had a passion for pizza. And while he still indulges his first love with monthly sell-out dough nights at the chipboard-festooned space, nowadays it's quality coffee that gets his pulse racing.

The Haxby hangout is the second edition in The Curious chronicles and has been luring tourists and locals from York to its neighbouring town since March 2017.

Just like the original Easingwold shop, beans are roasted in small batches by York Coffee Emporium and ground to order for an impeccably perky cup. Try the bespoke blend as a split shot to compare the coffee's flavour notes both black and when lavished with steamed milk.

TIP CHECK FACEBOOK FOR DEETS ON POP-UP PIZZA NIGHTS

The ever-changing array of cakes and traybakes provide excellent grazing material if you're settling into one of the comfy chairs with a cafetiere. A bite-sized chunk of brownie comes as standard with every brew and makes the perfect post-lunch pick-me-up following the belly-busting Curious Platter.

ESTABLISHED
2017

KEY ROASTER
York Coffee Emporium

BREWING METHODS
Espresso, french press

MACHINE
Cimbali M39

GRINDER
Faema MD3000

OPENING HOURS
Mon-Fri
7.30am-5pm
Sat 8.30am-4pm
Sun 9.30am-3pm

Gluten FREE

BEANS AVAILABLE INSTORE

ALTERNATIVE MILK

WIFI

CYCLE FRIENDLY

OUTDOOR seating

FAMILY Friendly

DISABLED ACCESS

BRING YOUR OWN Cup

www.curiouscoffee.co   01904 765158

@thecuriouscoffeecompany   @curiouscoffeed   @thecuriouscoffeecompany

BREW & BROWNIE

5 Museum Street, York, North Yorkshire, YO1 7DT

Seducing passersby with its decadent window display of golden cinnamon swirls, plump scones and impeccably layered sponge cakes since 2013, Brew & Brownie upped its baking game in June 2017 (much to the delight of diet-dodging locals) when it welcomed a dedicated bake shop to the fold.

Located two doors down Museum Street from the original outpost, the bakery has taken the heat off Brew & Brownie's busy little kitchen by kneading, rolling and decorating the bill of carb-based beauties that crowd the cafe's counter.

VISIT FOR COFFEE; STAY FOR A HEFTY HUNK OF MOCHA CAKE

This fresh addition means the kitchen team can focus on fashioning the towering pancakes which are partly responsible for the lengthy queue for a table on weekends. Whether you indulge in an American-style brunch or choose the thoroughly British black pudding stack, it's worth the wait.

Fuelling all this feasting is a cracking espresso blend from Allpress – there's usually a second option from the roastery on batch brew too.

ESTABLISHED
2013

KEY ROASTER
Allpress
Espresso

BREWING METHODS
Espresso,
AeroPress,
batch brew

MACHINE
La Marzocco
Linea PB

GRINDER
Victoria Arduino
Mythos One

OPENING HOURS
Mon-Sat
9am-5pm
Sun
9.30am-4pm

Gluten FREE

BEANS
AVAILABLE
INSTORE

ALTE
RNA
TIVE
MILK

WIFI

FAMILY
FRIENDLY

BRING
YOUR OWN
Cup.

www.brewandbrownie.com   01904 647420

Brew & Brownie   @brewandbrownie   @brewandbrownie

BURR COFFEE

5 Lendal, York, North Yorkshire, YO1 8AQ

Just a few doors away from some of the big coffee chains and close to Minster Gardens and York Library, this proud indie is showing the heavyweights how a decent cup of coffee is done.

Teaming up with Leeds' North Star for its beans, Burr is brewing a killer line-up of filters and a knockout flat white, turning the coffee drinkers of York to the good stuff – one shot at a time.

THE HOT CHOC IS A MUST – CHOOSE FROM DARK, MILK OR WHITE

You won't find any factory farmed cakes accompanying the coffee here either. There's always a haul of homemade bakes to battle over – try and come to a decision between a whoopee pie, fruit scone, raspberry brownie or lusciously layered millionaire's shortbread.

The team have also got savoury sustenance covered; the kitchen is famed for its superfood salad bar where huge bowls of creative vegetable dishes and grain glories are yours for the choosing.

ESTABLISHED
2006

KEY ROASTER
North Star
Coffee Roasters

BREWING METHOD
Espresso,
AeroPress, V60

MACHINE
Dalla Corte
Mina

GRINDER
Mahlkonig
K30 Vario

OPENING HOURS
Mon-Sat
8am-5pm
Sun 9am-4pm

www.burrcoffee.co.uk | 01904 644410

SPRING ESPRESSO – LENDAL

21 Lendal, York, North Yorkshire, YO1 8AQ

'**R**ighteous and true since 2006' is the proudly displayed declaration emblazoned across Spring Espresso's window.

And while the original coffee shop has done great service in expertly caffeinating its loyal customers for over a decade, this Lendal little sister only joined the party two years ago.

Pop in for an expertly prepared pre-work caffeine fix – it's just a quick dash from York train station – or make it a long 'n' lazy lunch with a V60 pourover of the latest beans from guest roaster Workshop.

A board by the bar gives visitors the low-down on the espresso from London's Square Mile – the seasonal Red Brick blend is particularly popular for its sweet hit of blood orange, toasted hazelnut and vanilla finish.

SEATS FILL UP FAST, SO POOTLE OVER EARLY TO BAG A BANQUETTE

Once you've decided between the beans, you'll need a few more minutes to consider the cakes and biscuits piled high behind the glass counter. Or, if you're sporting a healthy appetite, tuck into a stack of bouncy pancakes served with bacon, pecans and maple syrup.

ESTABLISHED
2016

KEY ROASTER
Square Mile
Coffee Roasters

BREWING METHOD
Espresso, V60,
AeroPress,
cold drip

MACHINE
Synesso
Hydra MVP

GRINDER
Victoria Arduino
Mythos One
Clima Pro,
Mahlkonig EK43

OPENING HOURS
Mon-Sun
8am-6pm

 Gluten FREE

 BEANS AVAILABLE INSTORE

 ALTERNATIVE MILK

 CYCLE FRIENDLY

 BRING YOUR OWN Cup.

 COFFEE COURSES

www.springespresso.co.uk   01904 656556

@springespressolendal   @springespresso   @springespresso

— MANCHESTER —
COFFEE
FESTIVAL

3-4/11/18

VICTORIA WAREHOUSE
MANCHESTER

Tickets at CUPNORTH.CO.UK

 @CUPNORTH

TALKS
TASTING
BREWING
ROASTERS
WORKSHOPS
COMPETITION

BROUGHT TO YOU BY:

THE ATTIC AND CAFE HARLEQUIN

2 Kings Square, York, North Yorkshire, YO1 8BH

Two floors. Three shop concepts. Multiple brew methods. Countless Has Bean single origins to choose from. It's a safe bet that even the most seasoned coffee connoisseur will find something novel at The Attic and Cafe Harlequin in York.

The top floor of the historic townhouse is where the coffee sorcery goes down, with bountiful beans crafted into all manner of brews by the knowledgeable brethren of baristas. Headed up by owner Gordon Howell, this has been the place to explore extraordinary caffeine in York for over a decade.

CHECK OUT THE NEW SELECTION OF TEAS AND COLD COFFEES

Downstairs deals in scones, sarnies and salads – made using locally sourced ingredients – and still pulls an exemplary espresso if The Attic is closed on your visit.

Want to recreate the magic in your kitchen? Become a home brew hotshot and fill your tote at the retail section – the coffee shop stocks a wealth of equipment and Has Bean coffee to-go, too.

ESTABLISHED
2006

KEY ROASTER
Has Bean Coffee

BREWING METHODS
Espresso, V60, Kalita Wave, Clever Dripper, Chemex, EK shots, AeroPress, french press

MACHINE
Dalla Corte Mina, Dalla Corte Evo 1

GRINDER
Dalla Corte, Mahlkonig EK43

OPENING HOURS
Mon-Sat
10am-4pm
Sun
10.30am-3.30pm

www.harlequinyork.com   01904 630631

@theatticgallerycoffeebar   @harlequinyork   @theatticcoffeebar

MAP Nº 84. SPRING ESPRESSO – FOSSGATE

45 Fossgate, York, North Yorkshire, YO1 9TF

Merchants Quarter is indie central in York, so it's no surprise to find a Spring Espresso outpost among the melange of artisan businesses and quirky stores thronging Fossgate.

Owner Steve Dyson knows a thing or two about a seriously good cup of Joe, as not only did he set up one of the city's first speciality coffee shops, he's also sat on the UKBC sensory judging panel for the past six years and been a semi-finalist in the comp four times.

TIP CHECK OUT SPRING'S SISTER CAFE ON LENDAL STREET

You'll often find Steve – along with his bevy of keen baristas – slinging shots on the slick Synesso Hydra (all the way from Seattle, don'tcha know) and serving homemade eight-hour cold drip coffee behind the bar at the bustling cafe.

Steve recommends pairing the house Square Mile flat white with a bostock – a house-baked brioche slice that's chock-full of almonds, juicy raspberries and blueberries.

ESTABLISHED
2011

KEY ROASTER
Square Mile
Coffee Roasters

BREWING METHOD
Espresso, V60,
AeroPress,
cold drip

MACHINE
Synesso Hydra

GRINDER
Victoria Arduino
Mythos One
Clima Pro,
Mahlkonig
EK43 S

OPENING HOURS
Mon-Sun
8am-6pm

 Gluten FREE

 BEANS AVAILABLE INSTORE

 ALTERNATIVE MILK

 CYCLE FRIENDLY

 OUTDOOR seating

 BRING YOUR OWN cup

COFFEE COURSES

www.springespresso.co.uk   01904 627730

 @springespressofossgate   @springespresso   @springespresso

MAP 85.

THE FOSSGATE SOCIAL

25 Fossgate, York, North Yorkshire, YO1 9TA

Sharing a street with a league of incredible indie businesses, The Fossgate Social sits at the heart of York's cultural quarter.

The sociable spot lives a double life. By day, the exposed brick walls, log burner and solid wood decor channel cosy cafe vibes, while beer pumps and overhead hanging wine glasses hint at Fossgate's alter ego as a buzzy bar serving craft beer, premium spirits and cocktails to night-time revellers – as well as kickass coffee for those more partial to brews than booze.

TIP BOOK FOSSGATE'S BLUE VELVET LOUNGE FOR YOUR NEXT PARTY OR EVENT

Hit the espresso martinis a little hard on your after-hours visit? Check back the next day for a reviving cup of something caffeinated. North Star's single origin beans provide sweet salvation from night-before antics and a pint-sized garden provides fresh air sipping.

And if you're in need of further revival, you'll find a good stock of beans to take home and cure any lingering hangovers.

ESTABLISHED
2014

ALSO ROASTED
North Star
Coffee Roasters

BREWING METHOD
Espresso,
Chemex

MACHINE
La Marzocco
Linea PB

GRINDER
Mazzer x 2

OPENING HOURS
Mon-Sat
9am-12.30am
Sun
10am-11.30pm

www.thefossgatesocial.com   01904 628692

f @thefossgatesocial   @fossgatesocial   @fossgatesocial

HOXTON NORTH

1 Royal Parade, Harrogate, North Yorkshire, HG1 2SZ

Head to Harrogate's Royal Parade to experience the kind of relaxed coffee culture you'd expect to encounter in the cooler quarters of Sydney, Melbourne or London.

The clean and design-led vibe of this smart coffee hangout reflects owners Timothy and Victoria Bosworth's desire to create a hip bar in their hometown of Harrogate.

TIP CHECK OUT THE RANGE OF QUALITY CRAFT GINS BEHIND THE BAR

Offering a warm welcome and ethically sourced coffee – courtesy of Cornwall's Origin and London's Volcano – Hoxton certainly hits capital city standards when it comes to the speciality served from its wooden bar.

Equal care goes into the epic brunches: 'traditional', 'vegan', 'dairy' and 'gluten-free' smatter the seasonal menu which champions small-scale producers.

Buzzing from dawn 'til dusk, this laid-back cafe transforms into a bar from midday, when a mixed crowd congregates to swap stories and imbibe organic, natural and biodynamic wines, craft beers and spirits.

ESTABLISHED
2013

KEY ROASTER
Origin Coffee Roasters

BREWING METHOD
Espresso

MACHINE
La Marzocco Linea PB

GRINDER
Victoria Arduino Mythos One

OPENING HOURS
Mon-Thu
8.30am-9pm
Fri 8.30am-11pm
Sat 9.30am-11pm
Sun 9.30am-5pm

 Gluten FREE

BEANS AVAILABLE INSTORE

ALTERNATIVE MILK

 WIFI

 OUTDOOR seating

 FAMILY friendly

 DISABLED ACCESS

www.hoxtonnorth.com   01423 564061

@hoxtonnorth   @hoxtonnorth   @hoxtonnorth

STARLING INDEPENDENT BEER & COFFEE HOUSE

47 Oxford Street, Harrogate, North Yorkshire, HG1 1PW

It may have emerged as a hatchling just a year ago but this starling's reputation is soaring among Harrogate's high-flyers, having already bagged a pair of awards for its enticing combo of craft beer, speciality coffee and heavenly homemade grub.

Visiting lovebirds cooing over a cuppa are made as welcome as a flight of friends ready for a round of G&Ts at this north Yorkshire perch. Foodies flock here too for the porridge, pizza and poutine – not forgetting the chance to get their beaks around the utterly indulgent affogato.

Great Taste award winning Under Milk Wood beans, roasted by Huddersfield's Dark Woods, are expertly crafted into indulgently caramely espresso on the La Marzocco.

NITRO COLD BREW, COURTESY OF MINOR FIGURES, HITS THE SPOT

Want to switch things up? Keep your peepers peeled for three to four guest beans appearing on V60, especially the Ethiopian greens that have been aged in bourbon barrels before roasting by the gang at Dark Woods.

ESTABLISHED
2017

KEY ROASTER
Dark Woods Coffee

BREWING METHODS
Espresso, V60, nitro

MACHINE
La Marzocco Linea PB

GRINDER
Mazzer Super Jolly, Mahlkonig EK43

OPENING HOURS
Mon-Wed
9am-10pm
Thu-Sat
9am-11pm
Sun 10am-9pm

www.starlinghgte.co.uk   01423 531310

@starlinghgte   @starlinghgte   @starlinghgte

88. BALTZERSEN'S

22 Oxford Street, Harrogate, North Yorkshire, HG1 1PU

The pro team at Baltzersen's have upped their coffee game further this year: upgrading the grinder, investing in a Puqpress precision tamper and adding a killer collection of new brewing kit to the bar.

It's not just the latest tech taking the Scandi/Yorkshire caffeine experience to the next level either, as the canned cold brew from Dishforth's FITCH and speciality beans from North Star and Maude also contribute to the delights of a trip to the Harrogate hangout.

TIP BRING YOUR KEEPCUP – BALTZERSEN'S DITCHED DISPOSABLES IN MAY 2018

While the coffee is constantly evolving, the Nordic-inspired, Yorkshire-sourced foodie offering remains faithful to owner Paul Rawlinson's roots. Savoury seekers can get their fill from a menu of traditional open sandwiches served with potato salad (try the meatball number with fried onions, melted cheese and lingonberry jam) before giving in to the homemade cinnamon buns and freshly pressed gluten-free waffles with vanilla whipped cream.

Foodie thrills continue after hours at the monthly taco night, FredagsTaco. *'Yes, tacos are a thing in Scandinavia,'* assures Paul. Now you know.

ESTABLISHED
2012

KEY ROASTER
Multiple roasters

BREWING METHOD
Espresso, drip

MACHINE
La Marzocco Linea PB

GRINDER
Anfim SP II

OPENING HOURS
Mon-Sat
8am-5pm
Sun 9am-4pm

www.baltzersens.co.uk   01423 202363

@baltzersens   @baltzersens   @baltzersens

MAP 89.

HARROGATE

NO35 HARROGATE

35 Cheltenham Crescent, Harrogate, North Yorkshire, HG1 1DH

What started as a passion project for friends Nino, Rob and Jamie has become a hotspot for quality coffee in Harrogate in less than a year.

Fuelled by a fascination for brilliant beans and banging bagels, the trio took a hands-on approach to craft their dream dough-and-'spro stop, tearing down plasterboard to expose the building's original brick interior and crafting a slick white bar for their Sanremo centrepiece.

While the order of the day is the Londoner bagel (avocado and prosciutto), millennials flock, phones in hand, to sip and pap the 'world's most Instagrammable coffee'. The Coffee Cone – a flat white served in a chocolate-lined waffle cone and finished with a rosetta – is the house special.

TIP NO35 IS SUPER DOG FRIENDLY – THE TEAM EVEN FEATURE AN 'INSTA PUP OF THE WEEK'

Don't worry, this isn't all mouth and no trousers: house beans are expertly provided by North Star, while a monthly changing guest spot features speciality roasting finds from across the UK.

ESTABLISHED
2017

KEY ROASTER
North Star
Coffee Roasters

BREWING METHOD
Espresso, V60,
Chemex,
AeroPress

MACHINE
Sanremo
Verona TCS

GRINDER
Sanremo
SR70 Evo

OPENING HOURS
Mon-Fri
7am-5pm
Sat 9am-5pm
Sun 10am-4pm

www.no35harrogate.coffee

@No35Harrogate @no35harrogate @no35harrogate

BEAN & BUD

MAP

14 Commercial Street, Harrogate, North Yorkshire, HG1 1TY

Putting lip-smackingly good single origins in the spotlight has been Bean & Bud's aim since it opened in 2010, and it's earned the Harrogate hangout two Best Coffee Shop accolades so far.

The experienced and friendly team are passionate about their craft, and will happily talk beans and brewing methods with budding baristas and curious coffee folk who drop in to the colourful cafe.

Hone your caffeine cognisance at one of the regular cupping events and coffee courses or, if you'd rather leave the pourovers to the professionals, explore new roasts via the fortnightly rotating guest spot.

KEEP 'EM PEELED FOR THEMED POP-UP DINING EVENTS

Dedication to speciality extends to whole-leaf tea at Bean & Bud (hence the name) and the award winning line-up includes rare and wonderful blends such as Wuyi Mountain Oolong.

Breakfast, lunch and all-day delights also draw on a jet-setting tour of world flavours – pair your espresso with a fresh-from-the-oven pastel de nata.

2010

Campbell & Syme

Espresso, V60, Chemex, AeroPress, Kalita Wave

La Marzocco Strada EP

Mythos, Mahlkonig K30, Mahlkonig Tanzania

Mon-Sat
8am-5pm
Sun 10am-4pm

www.beanandbud.co.uk   01423 508200

@beanandbud   @beanandbud   @beanandbud

THE HEDGEROW

Station Road, Threshfield, North Yorkshire, BD23 5BP

It's a wonder that, between fashioning fabulous floral arrangements and running a flower school, mother-and-daughter duo Wendy and Heather Hutchinson find time to craft speciality grade coffee.

But it's all in a day's work for the family team at Hedgerow, and it's what makes the unique florist/coffee shop mash-up a scent-sational (ahem) experience.

Wendy takes care of the flora, while Heather has been growing the speciality side of the business since returning to her hometown in 2014. A recent skill-enhancing trip to Berlin where she spent time at The Barn has also helped Heather's coffee offering blossom.

SOMETHING SAVOURY? TRY A CHEESE SCONE WITH MERCERS CHILLI JAM

Lancaster roaster Atkinsons provides the mainstay beans for the hopper, while Coopers is currently hitting up the guest slot for those looking to try something different.

Select your caffeinated cup of choice, nab a slice of homemade cake, then settle in the refurbed courtyard and bask in the beauty of the blooms.

1990

Atkinsons
Coffee Roasters

Espresso,
batch filter

Nuova Simonelli
Aurelia II

Nuova Simonelli
Mythos One

Tue-Fri
9am-5pm
Sat 9am-4pm

Gluten
FREE

BEANS
AVAILABLE
INSTORE

ALTE
RNA
TIVE
MILK

CYCLE
FRIENDLY

OUTDOOR
Seating

FAMILY
FRIENDLY

DISABLED
ACCESS

BRING
YOUR OWN
Cup.

www.the-hedgerow.co.uk   01765 752293

@thehedgerowthreshfeild   @the_hedgerow

92. LAY OF THE LAND

Kings Mill Lane, Settle, North Yorkshire, BD24 9BS

This is a one-stop shop for foliage, fodder and fantastic coffee. Hidden away among leafy plants and luscious pots in the heart of a bonsai-sized garden centre, you'll stumble upon a light and bright, contemporary coffee shop with an oak-tree sized reputation.

Potter around the zany assortment of gardening paraphernalia then pop in for a Casa Espresso single origin coffee – beans are switched up every couple of weeks so there's usually something new to try via espresso or AeroPress.

Chef James Lay, who trained at Michelin starred Northcote in Langho, recently launched a new menu which has had gardeners and foodies alike raving about the homemade pork pies, scotch eggs and sweet potato falafel.

DON'T MISS MEG'S SPECTACULAR SIX-LAYER CAKES AT THE WEEKEND

James makes everything in house – from ketchup and salad dressing to daily baked scones and jewel-pink gin and beetroot-cured salmon – so you can be confident the food and coffee reach the same lofty heights.

ESTABLISHED
2015

KEY ROASTER
Casa Espresso

BREWING METHOD
Espresso,
AeroPress,
pourover

MACHINE
Sanremo
Verona RS

GRINDER
Sanremo
SR70 Evo

OPENING HOURS
Mon-Sat
9am-4pm
Sun 10am-3pm

 Gluten FREE

 BEANS AVAILABLE INSTORE

 ALTERNATIVE MILK

 WIFI

 CYCLE FRIENDLY

 OUTDOOR seating

 FAMILY FRIENDLY

 DISABLED ACCESS

 BRING YOUR OWN cup

www.layoftheland.co.uk   01729 824247
@layofthelandsettle   @lay_of_the_land   @layoftheland_settle

EXCHANGE COFFEE COMPANY – SKIPTON

10 Gargrave Road, Skipton, North Yorkshire, BD23 1PJ

There's more than a whiff of nostalgia about this charming specialist coffee roaster and tea merchant in Skipton. After all, there are few things in life as pleasingly retro as warming yourself next to an original fireplace while inhaling the aroma of freshly roasted coffee and watching staff weigh out loose leaves and beans.

The roasters, who expertly develop green beans on the Probat GN12, are following a hallowed tradition – Exchange took over the building from Charles A Hallas who roasted here until the mid-1990s.

IN WARMER WEATHER SIT ALFRESCO WITH AN ICED COFFEE OR FRAPPE

Downstairs you'll be giddy with choice as you peruse shelves heaving with coffees and teas, among which you'll discover rare gems like La Candelilla Monte Canet, a micro lot, honey-processed coffee from Costa Rica.

To fully appreciate the antiques and ambience, head upstairs and relax in the recently opened coffee house. Take your pick from more than 100 coffees and teas, hot chocolates, soft drinks, smoothies, cakes and tea breads.

ESTABLISHED
1997

KEY ROASTER
Exchange Coffee Company

BREWING METHOD
Espresso, Clever Dripper, french press

MACHINE
Expobar G10

GRINDER
Mahlkonig K30

OPENING HOURS
Mon, Wed-Sat
9am-4.30pm

Gluten FREE

BEANS AVAILABLE / INSTORE

ALTERNATIVE MILK

WIFI

CYCLE FRIENDLY

OUTDOOR SEATING

FAMILY FRIENDLY

BRING YOUR OWN CUP

COFFEE COURSES

www.exchangecoffee.co.uk   01756 795649

@exchangecoffeecompany   @exchange_coffee   @exchange_coffee

Great coffee comes from great beans. Great milk comes from cows given the freedom to graze on open pasture. That's why baristas love to use Stephensons milk. And we love chatting to our customers about latte art, and how they are helping to sustain our local rural communities.

So call Chris on 01524 388699 to join our herd.

www.stephensonsdairy.co.uk
T. 01524 388688
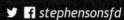 stephensonsfd

BEAN LOVED

17 Otley Street, Skipton, North Yorkshire, BD23 1DY

Rather than serving beans from many different roasteries, Bean Loved is rather purist and only brews coffee using Dark Woods roasts.

'We work closely with the Huddersfield roastery and want to share our signature blend with the people of Skipton,' explains Bean Loved owner Wes Bond.

The blend in question is hand roasted in small batches and you won't find it on filter at the Otley Street spot as Wes believes espresso best complements the complex flavour of these beans.

THE SALTED CARAMEL ICED LATTE IS SERIOUSLY INDULGENT

The team are equally as thoughtful about the food, and source as many ingredients as possible from within Yorkshire. Each day, chefs make hearty soups and seasonal breakfasts from scratch, while cakes are sourced from a line-up of local bakeries.

To celebrate over a decade of 'spro slinging, Bean Loved recently expanded to make the space even more comfortable and roomy to squeeze in all those regulars who have made this cathedral to caffeine their home from home.

ESTABLISHED
2007

KEY ROASTER
Dark Woods Coffee

BREWING METHOD
Espresso

MACHINE
La Marzocco FB80

GRINDER
Mythos One Clima Pro

OPENING HOURS
Mon-Fri
7.30am-5pm
Sat 8am-5pm
Sun 9am-5pm

 Gluten FREE

 BEANS AVAILABLE INSTORE

 ALTERNATIVE MILK

 WIFI

 CYCLE FRIENDLY

 OUTDOOR seating

 FAMILY FRIENDLY

DISABLED ACCESS

 BRING YOUR OWN Cup

www.beanloved.co.uk   01756 791534

@beanlovedskipton   @beanloved   @beanloved

95. STEEP & FILTER

14 Otley Street, Skipton, North Yorkshire, BD23 1DZ

The new kid on the Skipton coffee block may have only opened in February 2018, but this eco-conscious cafe is already putting its ethics into action.

With a focus on reducing waste and building connections with local suppliers and small businesses, owner Michael Jennings has created a specialist coffee shop which is also environmentally savvy.

'We want to push the current speciality coffee scene and eco-friendly ethos,' explains Michael. *'We also hope to become a hub for the Skipton community.'*

The result is an aesthetically pleasing space serving expertly prepared speciality alongside an exclusively veggie and vegan foodie offering. House faves include smoky squash, spinach and za'atar quiche, and smashed avo with chilli, mint and feta.

TIP CHECK OUT THE SEASONAL WALL MURALS, DESIGNED AND PAINTED BY LOCAL ARTISTS

In the hopper you'll find beans from North Star, with a Saturday takeover showcasing a single origin from the Leeds roaster. Plans are afoot, too, for regular guest espressos from further afield, so keep 'em peeled for new and noteworthy roasts.

ESTABLISHED
2018

KEY ROASTER
North Star
Coffee Roasters

BREWING METHOD
Espresso

MACHINE
La Marzocco
Linea PB

GRINDER
Fiorenzato
F64 Evo

OPENING HOURS
Mon, Wed-Sat
8am-4.30pm
Tue 8am-3.30pm
Sun 9am-3.30pm

Gluten FREE

ALTERNATIVE MILK

WIFI

CYCLE FRIENDLY

FAMILY FRIENDLY

DISABLED ACCESS

01756 795797

Steep & Filter @steepandfilter @steepandfilter

MAP 96

SIFT: CAFE & BAKERY

11 Manor Square, Otley, Leeds, West Yorkshire, LS21 3AP

It's impossible to pass Sift's attention-grabbingly gorgeous building without admiring the Grade II-listed former bank, but what really deserve your full attention are the towering cakes, kickass coffee and Instagram opportunities that await inside.

Inspired by a love of cafe culture, owner Rosie Crabbe has created a cheerful cafe full of flora, fauna and funky patterns. It's all too easy to kick back and relax here. Nab a sunny window seat for prime people-watching opps and take time over an expertly pulled Dark Woods espresso or London Fog – the love child of earl grey tea and chai latte.

TIP DON'T LEAVE WITHOUT A TRIP TO THE FAMOUS FLAMINGO LOO (TRUST US!)

The newly expanded food menu is completely veggie and totally delicious, with soups, tarts and sandwiches all crafted from colourful local produce.

Your session will inevitably end with a sweet wedge of homemade cake. We recommend the chocolate and peanut butter confection which is more than just a head turner: it delivers on taste too.

ESTABLISHED
2017

KEY ROASTER
Dark Woods Coffee

BREWING METHOD
Espresso

MACHINE
La Marzocco Linea PB

GRINDER
Cimbali Magnum

OPENING HOURS
Tue-Fri
9am-4pm
Sat 9am-5pm
Sun 10am-4pm

 Gluten FREE

 BEANS AVAILABLE INSTORE

 ALTERNATIVE MILK

 WIFI

 FAMILY FRIENDLY

 DISABLED ACCESS

 BRING YOUR OWN Cup

www.siftotley.com

f @siftotley　　@siftotley　　@siftotley

SALAMI & CO.

MAP 7

10 Market Place, Otley, West Yorkshire, LS21 3AQ

If you love coffee as much as you love your hound, the husband and wife team at Salami & Co have created the ideal hangout where you can drink quality caffeine with a four-legged friend in tow.

With their two dachshunds (Salami and Bagel) by their side, the couple opened this dog-friendly spot in 2016. It's bright and airy with fresh decor, bespoke fittings and lots of natural light flooding in.

TIP ALL OF THE CAKES – AND CANINE SNACKS – ARE CRAFTED IN HOUSE

Top of the must-try list is the house blend created with Casa Espresso, which is excellent as a cappuccino or sipped straight as espresso. Roasts from Maude and Dark Arts make guest appearances too, while in summer the Frank and Earnest nitro cold brew is a hit with weary walkers in need of cooling caffeinated refreshment.

The modern menu changes seasonally and showcases pastries sourced from Dumouchel in Garforth, cheese from The Courtyard Dairy in Settle and sourdough crafted by the Leeds Bread Co-op.

On warm days, an affogato is a must – choose from hazelnut and rose or chocolate and orange blossom ice cream. There's also a menu for four-legged friends, featuring handmade pupcakes and biscuit bones.

ESTABLISHED
2016

KEY ROASTER
Multiple roasters

BREWING METHOD
Espresso, V60, nitro, batch brew

MACHINE
Sanremo Verona RS

GRINDER
Sanremo SR50

OPENING HOURS
Mon, Wed-Sat
8am-6pm
Sun
8am-4.30pm

Gluten FREE

BEANS AVAILABLE INSTORE

ALTERNATIVE MILK

WIFI

DISABLED ACCESS

BRING YOUR OWN CUP

www.salamiandco.com   01943 968207

@salamiandco   @salamiandco   @salamiandco

BLOOMFIELD SQUARE

28-30 Gay Lane, Otley, Leeds, West Yorkshire, LS21 1BR

Dabbling in both lattes and letterpress, Tony Wright and Emma Thorpe like to do things a little differently at Otley's Bloomfield Square.

While Emma takes care of the cafe's kooky interiors, Tony leads the creative courses on the Victorian printing press and orchestrates a band of skilled baristas from the wood-decked brew bar.

The unique space attracts an equally eclectic clientele. You'll find both lycra-clad cyclists and weary dog walkers bopping along to ballads by old-school crooners and settling down for a North Star fix next to floor-to-ceiling artwork.

LOCKS AND SAFE SPOTS TO STORE BIKES MAKE THIS A CYCLING HOTSPOT

Health freaks will enjoy the golden hit of a turmeric latte, while veg-centric foodies can get their fill from the vegan-friendly menu which features seasonal post-ride pick-me-ups.

Talks from local sporting legends, supper clubs and live music gigs are just a few of the after-hours events on Bloomfield's busy line-up.

ESTABLISHED
2016

KEY ROASTER
North Star
Coffee Roasters

BREWING METHOD
Espresso,
V60, AeroPress

MACHINE
La Marzocco
Linea PB

GRINDER
Mahlkonig K30
ES, Mazzer Luigi

OPENING HOURS
Tue-Thu
9am-4pm
Fri-Sat
9am-5pm
Sun 10am-4pm

Gluten FREE

BEANS AVAILABLE
INSTORE

ALTERNATIVE MILK

WIFI

CYCLE FRIENDLY

FAMILY FRIENDLY

BRING YOUR OWN CUP

www.bloomfieldsquare.co.uk   01943 463683

@bloomfieldsquare   @bloomfieldsqr   @bloomfield_square

DEVELOPED WITH BARISTAS FOR BARISTAS

- Perfect for latte art
- No added sugar
- Cholesterol free, low fat alternative to milk
- 30% less calories than skimmed & regular soy milk

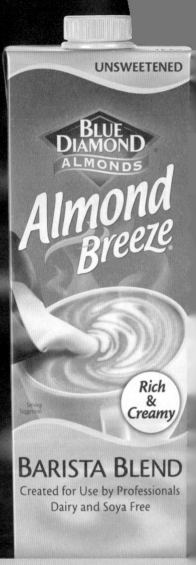

UNSWEETENED

BLUE DIAMOND
ALMONDS

Almond Breeze

Serving Suggestion

Rich & Creamy

BARISTA BLEND
Created for Use by Professionals
Dairy and Soya Free

Baristas know their coffee better than anyone. That's why we got baristas to help us make our new, low calorie Almond Breeze® Barista Blend. It's deliciously creamy and frothy, making it perfect for the world's finest coffee. And because it's an almond drink, it's dairy free and soya free

For more information & stockists visit **bluediamondalmonds.co.uk**

MAP 99.

TAMBOURINE COFFEE

38 Bingley Road, Saltaire, Shipley, West Yorkshire, BD18 4RU

Couples relaxing over a cuppa rub shoulders with laptop tappers and kids scrawling on blackboards at this welcome-to-all caffeinated refuge in Saltaire.

Super chilled vibes, artwork-adorned walls and a healthy roster of family-friendly events come together to fulfil Tambourine's mission to make coffee culture accessible to the whole community.

TIP VEGANS, TAKE NOTE: THE LOCALLY MADE CAKES AND BROWNIES ARE WORTH THE VISIT ALONE

Leeds-roasted North Star beans share shelf space with an ever-rotating array of roasts from Dark Woods, Maude, Girls Who Grind and Casa Espresso.

'We like to switch it up to showcase what the speciality industry has to offer and to keep up with current trends,' says owner Chris Large. The guest filter is a great way to discover a new roaster, and you can pick up beans for further experimentation at home.

Drooling over a table-neighbour's brunch of sweetcorn fritters with bacon and halloumi is all part of the Tambourine experience so, if you missed out first time, be sure to schedule a return visit to get your chops around the house speciality.

ESTABLISHED
2017

KEY ROASTER
North Star
Coffee Roasters

BREWING METHOD
Espresso,
batch filter

MACHINE
Sanremo
Verona RS,
Moccamaster

GRINDER
Mahlkonig K30,
Sanremo SR50

OPENING HOURS
Mon-Fri
7.30am-5pm
Sat 8.30am-5pm
Sun 9am-4pm

Gluten FREE

BEANS AVAILABLE
INSTORE

ALTERNATIVE MILK

WIFI

CYCLE FRIENDLY

OUTDOOR seating

FAMILY FRIENDLY

DISABLED ACCESS

BRING YOUR OWN Cup

www.tambourinecoffee.co.uk | 01274 945870

@tambourinecoffe   @tambourinecoffee

BOWERY CAFE

MAP № 100.

54 Otley Road, Leeds, West Yorkshire, LS6 2AL

Happy birthday Bowery! This self-professed 'home of creativity' turns ten this year – and what a caffeine-fuelled decade of incredible artistry it's been.

Step inside the cathedral to craftsmanship (it's a cafe, studio, shop and gallery don'tcha know) and you may find yourself joining in with jewellery makers, waxing lyrical with writers or signing up for the sewing circle before imbibing a brew. And that barely scratches the surface of the veritable feast of workshops, events and courses on offer.

SNEAK A PEEK AT THE UPSTAIRS GALLERY WHICH SHOWCASES EMERGING ARTISTS

Fuelling all of the creativity is a cheery band of baristas and a hopper brimming with Allpress beans. Browse the range of prints, mags and greeting cards while the artful team fashion a rosetta atop silky espresso or a flavour-wheel-spinning drip filter.

Ready for edible refreshment? The kaleidoscopic array of smoothies, salads, open sarnies and homebaked cakes could inspire even the least imaginative caffeine tourist.

ESTABLISHED
2008

KEY ROASTER
Allpress
Espresso

BREWING METHODS
Espresso, drip

MACHINE
La Marzocco
Linea Classic

GRINDER
Mazzer Super
Jolly Timer

OPENING HOURS
Mon-Thu
8.30am-6.30pm
Fri-Sat
8.30am-6pm
Sun 10am-5pm

 Gluten FREE

 BEANS AVAILABLE / INSTORE

 ALTERNATIVE MILK

 WIFI

 OUTDOOR SEATING

 FAMILY FRIENDLY

 BRING YOUR OWN CUP

www.thebowery.org   01132 242284

@boweryleeds   @theboweryarts   @boweryleeds

HOUSE OF KOKO

62 Harrogate Road, Chapel Allerton, Leeds, West Yorkshire, LS7 4LA

The soft hiss of the steam wand, the quiet nattering of friends and an occasional sweet sigh elicited by the first sip of coffee: House of Koko's backing track is better than any Spotify playlist.

The cafe's cacophony of yellow and teal furnishings, parquet floors, geometric-patterned brew bar and wall of beans, books and retro bits to browse ensure visual pleasures are equally as inspiring.

TIP HOMEMADE BAKES WILL MAKE THE SWEET TOOTHED GO WEAK AT THE KNEES

On the food front, Koko specialises in bangin' brunch plates and was voted the Best Place to Eat in Chapel Allerton in the local CARA Awards 2016. Plump for the Full Vegan – a plant purist's alternative to the full English brekkie and a winner with both carnivores and new-wave herbies.

Exciting collabs are being cooked up, too: *'We let new indie businesses take over our menu for a day now and then,'* says owner Chris Ball.

The Koko brunch experience is kicked up a level with a supremely sippable single origin from Leeds' North Star – ask the baristas for their recommendations on V60.

ESTABLISHED
2015

KEY ROASTER
North Star
Coffee Roasters

BREWING METHODS
Espresso, V60

MACHINE
Astoria
Gloria AL3

GRINDER
Anfim,
Mazzer

OPENING HOURS
Mon-Fri
8am-5pm
Sat 9am-5pm
Sun 10am-4pm

 Gluten FREE

 BEANS AVAILABLE INSTORE

 ALTERNATIVE MILK

 WIFI

 OUTDOOR SEATING

 FAMILY FRIENDLY

 DISABLED ACCESS

 BRING YOUR OWN Cup

www.houseofkoko.com   01132 621808

@houseofkoko   @houseofkoko   @houseofkoko

EPISODE ONE

83 Great George Street, Leeds, West Yorkshire, LS1 3BR

Locate the little yellow door on Great George Street and – for now, anyway – you'll be in on one of Leeds' best kept secrets.

A newbie to the local coffee scene, Episode One is quickly earning itself an enviable rep. Dubbed 'The E1 Social Club', the bright space has a sociable community vibe with pops of yellow, a banging playlist and smiley staff.

TIP THE AUSSIE-INSPIRED MENU DEALS IN ALL-DAY BREKKIES

It's not all about the aesthetics either, as E1 converts claim the team are slinging some of the best coffee this side of the city. With guest espresso changing monthly, it's worth earmarking this one for a return visit.

Home brewers eager to take their hobby to the next level can sign up to one of the regular workshops which cover everything from barista basics and cupping to tasting – you can even customise your learning with a personalised session.

ESTABLISHED
2018

KEY ROASTER
Ozone Coffee
Roasters

BREWING METHOD
Espresso,
Chemex,
Bee House

MACHINE
Sanremo
Café Racer

GRINDER
Mythos One
Clima Pro,
Mahlkonig EK43

OPENING HOURS
Mon-Fri
7am-5pm
Sat 9am-5pm

www.episodecoffee.co.uk   01132 441971

@e1coffee   @e1coffee

STAGE ESPRESSO & BREWBAR

41 Great George Street, Leeds, West Yorkshire, LS1 3BB

Stage 1: source a stonking selection of hand-roasted, speciality beans. Stage 2: craft into banging brews via a cluster of different methods. Stage 3: add game-changing elements including a booze licence, beautiful brunch menu, drool-worthy homemade bakes and a growing roster of events. (Optional stage 4: place in-house beagle Copper by the door for maximum luring-in opportunities.)

BRING YOUR REUSABLE CUP FOR A 10 PER CENT DISCOUNT OFF YOUR TAKEAWAY

It looks like Stage Espresso is set for coffee shop success. Having only opened last year, this friendly bunch are already grabbing the attention of Leeds' caffeinated community.

Keen to showcase some of the finest speciality on offer, the gang's mainstay Union beans share counter space with an evolving line-up of guests – Maude, Taylor Street and Round Hill have all featured so far.

Whether you're stopping by for coffee and cake or an espresso to-go, quality craftsmanship is guaranteed as barista Matt won the Union Hand-Roasted Barista Championship 2017.

ESTABLISHED
2017

KEY ROASTER
Union Hand-Roasted Coffee

BREWING METHOD
Espresso, Kalita Wave, batch brew, Clever Dripper

MACHINE
La Marzocco Linea Classic

GRINDER
Mythos One Clima Pro, Mahlkonig EK43

OPENING HOURS
Mon-Fri
7.30am-5pm
Sat 9am-5pm

BEANS
AVAILABLE
INSTORE

ALTERNATIVE
MILK

WIFI

BRING
YOUR OWN
Cup.

COFFEE
COURSES

www.stagecoffee.com

@stagecoffee   @stagecoffee   @stagecoffeeleeds

104. LA BOTTEGA MILANESE – THE LIGHT

The Headrow, Leeds, West Yorkshire, LS1 8TL

Ever had a holiday where you wish you could capture the lifestyle and relive it once you're home? You're in luck if your vacation was of the Italian variety as this charming coffee shop serves a slice of Milan to Leeds' continental congregati.

'Our store mimics a typical Italian espresso bar atmosphere,' explains owner Alex Galantino. *'Tight, loud, and you can't escape us: you have to mingle. We offer escapism with no need to get on a plane – we are Milan!'*

TIP DON'T MISS FRIDAY DOUGHNUTS – ARRIVE EARLY BEFORE THEY FLY OUT THE DOOR

Since last year, Alex and team have turned up the heat to achieve a more authentic Milanese experience at the much-loved tavola calda. Elegant rebranding reflects Italian cafe culture, while an impending facelift will transport the city's brew crew to sunnier climes as they sip.

A best-of Italian menu – drool over daily made Sicilian cannoli – mixes it up with collabs with Yorkshire producers. It's complemented by La Classica espresso, a monthly guest and single origin decaf.

ESTABLISHED
2009

ROASTER
Dark Woods
Coffee

BREWING METHODS
Espresso,
batch filter

MACHINE
Faema E61

GRINDER
Mythos One
Clima Pro,
Cimbali
Magnum

OPENING HOURS
Mon-Thu
7.30am-8pm
Fri 7am-9pm
Sun 10am-7pm

Gluten FREE

BEANS AVAILABLE
INSTORE

ALTERNATIVE MILK

WIFI

DISABLED ACCESS

BRING YOUR OWN Cup

www.labottegamilanese.co.uk   01132 454242

@labottega.milanese   @bottegamilanese   @labottegamilanese

MAP 105.

LA BOTTEGA MILANESE – BOND COURT

2 Bond Court, Leeds, West Yorkshire, LS1 2JZ

Arrive early to bag a sunny seat at this not-so-secret suntrap in Leeds. The outdoor area is a sliver of continental cafe culture, where customers sprawl on deck chairs with specialist drinks (of the caffeinated or alcoholic variety) and indulge in a taste of legit Milanese life.

Tempting? It's not just the alfresco seating and light, airy indoor space that draw in the crowds – this lot serve a damn fine cup of coffee, too.

'We've been working with Damian at Dark Woods for years and are involved in every step – from choosing the bean to the roast profile,' says Italian owner Alex Galantino.

WATCH THIS SPACE FOR A SNAZZY NEW REFURB

'We tend to shortlist three blend variations each time we change, and get staff and customers to blind taste to decide the next house blend.'

A recent rebrand and new merch sets the gang apart in this speciality-blessed city – you won't find another spot quite like it for an authentic European experience.

ESTABLISHED
2014

KEY ROASTER
Dark Woods
Coffee

BREWING METHODS
Espresso, V60,
batch filter,
AeroPress

MACHINE
La Marzocco
Linea PB

GRINDER
Mythos One
Clima, Cimbali
Magnum

OPENING HOURS
Mon-Thu
7am-6pm
Fri 7am-7pm
Sat 9am-6pm
Sun 10am-5pm

Gluten FREE

BEANS AVAILABLE
INSTORE

ALTERNATIVE MILK

WIFI

CYCLE FRIENDLY

OUTDOOR seating

DISABLED ACCESS

BRING YOUR OWN Cup

www.labottegamilanese.co.uk   01132 431102

@labottega.milanese   @bottegamilanese   @labottegamilanese

106. OUT OF THE WOODS – WATER LANE

113 Water Lane, Leeds, West Yorkshire, LS11 5WD

Good things come in small packages. And at this particular find, nestled in a thriving urban village, you can behold Brown & Blond brownies, decadent cakes and freshly blended smoothies.

Sink into a squashy sofa and cast an eye down the weekly changing specials list (featuring ciabatta from OOTW's artisan allies at Leeds Bread Co-operative) for foodie fulfilment. Health seekers will find superfood solace in the granola and acai berry brekkie bowl.

The gang put local produce at the top of the shopping list for all this fab food: 'As much as we can get our hands on,' says owner Ross Stringer.

TIP DON'T MISS ROSS' HOMEMADE SECRET-RECIPE TOMATO CHUTNEY

And the coffee? Staple roasts are sourced from Yorkshire buddies Dark Woods, with a cracking guest bill including the likes of North Star, Press Coffee and Girls Who Grind.

Get your flat white fix pulled through the La Marzocco PB, opt for an in-demand batch brew or crack on with cold brew on sunny days.

ESTABLISHED
2006

KEY ROASTER
Dark Woods Coffee

BREWING METHOD
Espresso, batch brew, cold brew

MACHINE
La Marzocco PB

GRINDER
Mahlkonig K30

OPENING HOURS
Mon-Fri
7am-4pm

www.outofthewoods.me.uk   01132 448123

outofthewoodsuk   outofthewoodsuk   outofthewoodsuk

107. OUT OF THE WOODS – GRANARY WHARF

Watermans Place, Granary Wharf, Leeds, West Yorkshire, LS1 4GL

'**N**o canoodling' states the sign on the wall of this log-cabin-style lovely. Abstain from the smooching if you must but there's little chance you won't fall for Out of the Woods' Granary Wharf outpost.

Find a pew between the regular cycling and dog walking crowd, all fresh faced and finding caffeinated reward after invigorating canalside exercise, and settle in with a Dark Woods brew pulled through the La Spaziale machine.

TIP HEAD TO HOLBECK URBAN VILLAGE TO VISIT OOTW'S ORIGINAL PIT-STOP AT WATER LANE

Return trip? Plump for a North Star guest roast to sample something different – OOTW owner Ross and her band of baristas have only recently started serving batch brew, so give 'em the chance to show off the fresh filter kit.

Coffee is paired with satisfying sustenance such as oozy grilled cheese sarnies, seasonal soups and salads, as well as almighty home bakes to make sweet-toothed sojourners' mouths water.

ESTABLISHED
2010

KEY ROASTER
Dark Woods Coffee

BREWING METHOD
Espresso, batch brew

MACHINE
La Spaziale

GRINDER
Mahlkonig K30

OPENING HOURS
Mon-Fri
7am-4pm
Sat 9am-4pm

 Gluten FREE

 BEANS AVAILABLE / INSTORE

 ALTERNATIVE MILK

 WIFI

 CYCLE FRIENDLY

OUTDOOR seating

 DISABLED ACCESS

 BRING YOUR OWN Cup

www.outofthewoods.me.uk | 01132 454144

f @outofthewoodsuk @outofthewoodsuk @outofthewoodsuk

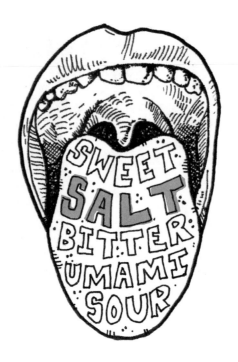

Don't be bland

For freakin' delicious marketing, creative design and publishing from experts in food, drink and hospitality, just add salt

01271 859299 | saltmedia.co.uk

LAYNES ESPRESSO

14-16 New Station Street, Leeds, West Yorkshire, LS1 5DL

The first call on any caffeine tour of Leeds, this northern coffee scene staple is just seconds from the train station and has welcomed visitors to the city with a stellar cup since 2011.

Scores of speciality pilgrims pile in to sample the beany offering and newly pimped menus, so Laynes made more room last year with an extension which has turned the coffee shop into one of the city's best-loved brunch spots.

Abuzz with friends debriefing over hot smoked salmon and eggs, and coffee folk getting their fill of savoury buckwheat pancakes, this uber hip hub certainly hasn't let speciality standards slip since upping the food offering.

VEGANS, THE PLANT-BASED FULL ENGLISH BREKKIE IS A GAME-CHANGER

House beans from London's Square Mile continue to share shelf space with a roll call of quality roasters such as Dark Woods, Round Hill, Five Elephant and Colonna. A split shot option lets you sample the latest espresso straight up and with milk, or go the whole kit and caboodle and sample via V60 and AeroPress.

ESTABLISHED
2011

KEY ROASTER
Square Mile
Coffee Roasters

BREWING METHOD
Espresso, V60,
AeroPress

MACHINE
Synesso MVP

GRINDER
Mythos One
Clima Pro,
Mahlkonig EK43

OPENING HOURS
Mon-Fri
7am-7pm
Sat-Sun
9am-6pm

 Gluten FREE

 BEANS AVAILABLE INSTORE

 ALTERNATIVE MILK

 WIFI

 FAMILY FRiENDLY

www.laynesespresso.co.uk   07828 823189

@laynesespresso   @laynesespresso   @laynesespresso

109. KAPOW COFFEE

46 The Calls, Leeds, West Yorkshire, LS2 7EY

This year the Kapow crew packed their tampers, stowed the Sanremo and loaded up their V60s for the big move ... next door.

Now based at number 46 The Calls, the gang's mission remains to serve the waterfront business district with exquisite espresso and perfect pourovers from the industrial-style indie space.

Sourcing and selling a selection of stonking beans from around the UK (we're talking North Star, Dark Woods, Horsham, Round Hill, Union, Rounton, Dark Arts ...), a quality cup is guaranteed.

HIT 'EM UP FROM 10-11AM OR 2-3PM FOR LOW PRICE SWIGGING DURING HAPPY HOUR

And it's no wonder there are so many loyal regulars: owner and manager Steve has a mind-bogglingly near-perfect memory of his customers' fave pours – just one example of how everyone feels welcome at Kapow.

Want to continue your caffeinated crawl? A ten minute stroll up the road will take you to Kapow's other well-worth-a-visit outpost – the three-storey artsy cafe and retail space within Thornton's Arcade.

ESTABLISHED
2013

KEY ROASTER
Multiple roasters

BREWING METHOD
Espresso, V60, AeroPress

MACHINE
Sanremo Amalfi Deluxe

GRINDER
Mahlkonig K30, Sanremo SR50

OPENING HOURS
Mon-Fri
7am-5pm

BEANS AVAILABLE INSTORE

ALTERNATIVE MILK

WIFI

CYCLE FRIENDLY

OUTDOOR SEATING

DISABLED ACCESS

BRING YOUR OWN CUP

www.kapowcoffee.co.uk

@kapow46thecalls @kapowcoffee @kapowcoffee

NORTH STAR COFFEE SHOP & GENERAL STORE

Unit 32, The Boulevard, Leeds Dock, Leeds, West Yorkshire, LS10 1PZ

Celebrating its first birthday in July 2018, North Star's Coffee Shop & General Store has quickly gained a reputation for great caffeine and community vibes in the Leeds Dock area.

Curious coffee folk get a peek at the roasting process via sliding glass doors which reveal the humming roastery space next door.

The textiles, textures and tropical plants throughout the light and airy shop are tokens of founders Alex and Holly Kragiopoulos' trips to origin over the years. Sample the bounty of their sourcing travels with the tasting flight or choose between five seasonal single origins on filter or the two own-roasted espresso options.

SWING BY ON A FRIDAY NIGHT FOR THE BEST COFFEE COCKTAILS IN TOWN

The gang are big on sensory pairings too, so the food is as considered as the exclusive micro lots. Noisette Bakehouse is North Star's neighbour and the two work together to match flavours of coffee to specific plates and bakes on the seasonal menu.

ESTABLISHED
2017

KEY ROASTER
North Star
Coffee Roasters

BREWING METHOD
Espresso,
Kalita Wave,
batch brew,
cold brew

MACHINE
La Marzocco
Linea PB

GRINDER
Mythos One
Clima Pro,
Mahlkonig EK43

OPENING HOURS
Mon-Thu
7.30am-5.30pm
Fri 7.30am-7pm
Sat 9am-5pm
Sun 10am-4pm

 MILK

 WIFI

www.northstarroast.co.uk   07725 144204

@northstarcoffeeshop   @northstarroast   @northstarcoffeeshop

MAP № 111.

SQUEEZE SANDWICHES AND SMOOTHIES

19 Crown Street, Hebden Bridge, West Yorkshire, HX7 8EH

Blending vibrant smoothies, building badass sarnies and dishing out a crowd-pleasing menu of Mexican greats alongside some slick espresso: Martha Howard squeezes a whole lotta deliciousness into her Hebden Bridge cafe.

But despite the locals cramming in to get their daily dose of Dark Woods' Crow Tree blend, Squeeze's exposed brick walls, floor-to-ceiling window and tall tables with stools create a feeling of space – even when there's not masses of it.

TIP PLANT-BASED PLEASURE SEEKERS CAN GET THEIR FILL FROM THE VEGAN MENU

If you're lucky enough to secure a spot on one of the comfy sofas, take it as an omen from the coffee gods and stick around to sample both the Huddersfield house beans and guest espresso from Lancaster roaster Atkinsons. Feeling wired? Coffee shakes can be soothed via the blender – the Green Goddess of apple, banana, ginger, lime, spinach and apple juice is particularly restorative.

Foodie thrills are catered for via Squeeze's freshly stacked sarnies and all-day Mexican brunch dishes. Check in early for a breakfast quesadilla of baked eggs, tomato, spinach, bacon, cheddar and cajun spices.

ESTABLISHED
2007

KEY ROASTER
Dark Woods Coffee

BREWING METHOD
Espresso

MACHINE
Cimbali

GRINDER
Mazzer, Ceado, Mini Ceado

OPENING HOURS
Mon-Sat
8.30am-4pm
Sun 10am-4pm

www.squeezehebden.co.uk 01422 471265

@squeezehebden @squeezehebden @squeezehebden

MAP 112.

ARCADE COFFEE & FOOD

9 Byram Arcade, Huddersfield, West Yorkshire, HD1 1ND

L aunched in December 2017 by school friends Jonny and Tommy (along with business partner Mark), this charming spot is the latest addition to Huddersfield's blooming coffee scene.

Slinging 'spros from local roaster Dark Woods and featuring guests from the likes of Maude and Girls Who Grind, the guys have all the goods to ensure you get a cracking cup of coffee.

Iced cold brew comes out in summer, while sickly-sweet syrups are swapped for a spoonful of Yorkshire honey in the line-up of winter warmers.

TIP VEGAN BREKKIE OPTIONS INCLUDE AWESOME AUBERGINE, BACON AND DILL FRITTERS

The foodie offering includes seasonal specials such as vegan bhaji burgers and steaming bowls of ramen, along with fruit-studded loaves and frosted cakes baked by Rosie in Otley.

Recently, Friday and Saturday opening hours have been extended to showcase a new menu of cocktails and craft beers; fuel your boozy brunch with a Red Snapper bloody mary made with rhubarb gin.

ESTABLISHED
2017

KEY ROASTER
Dark Woods Coffee

BREWING METHODS
Espresso, batch filter, cold brew

MACHINE
La Marzocco Linea Classic

GRINDER
Cimbali Magnum, Mahlkonig EK43

OPENING HOURS
Mon-Thu
8am-6pm
Fri 8am-10pm
Sat 9am-10pm
Sun 10am-4pm

01484 511148

@arcadecoffeefood   @rcadecoffeefood

MAP 113. # COFFEEVOLUTION

8 Church Street, Huddersfield, West Yorkshire, HD1 1DD

Keeping Huddersfield's caffeine levels expertly elevated for nearly 20 years, and serving bronzed beauties from sister company Bean Brothers since 2012, Coffeevolution was one of the first speciality shops in this part of the country.

You'll often find owner James at the end of Coffeevolution's busy bar, cupping the latest beans from his down-the-road roastery and chatting tasting notes with the league of regulars who frequent the bright 'n' bold shop.

The talented team are sharp on a multitude of brewing methods and always up for a quick run-down on the best way to serve your pick of the beans. And if you're looking to craft cafe-standard coffee at home, you'll find a healthy stock of beans and brewing equipment on sale.

TIP MORE THAN A CAFE, COFFEEVOLUTION DOUBLES UP AS HUDDERSFIELD'S CREATIVE HUB

We'd recommend sinking into one of the leather sofas, or plonking yourself down at a communal table, and breaking out a board game. If you're lucky, Smudge (the roaster's patterdale terrier) will come over and say hi – pooch-petting comes as an optional side with your piccolo.

ESTABLISHED
2000

KEY ROASTER
Bean Brothers
Coffee Company

BREWING METHOD
Espresso,
Chemex,
AeroPress,
V60, nitro,
Hario cold brew

MACHINE
La Marzocco
Linea MP

GRINDER
Anfim, Mazzer

OPENING HOURS
Mon-Fri
7am-7pm
Sat 8am-7pm
Sun 9am-6pm

 Gluten FREE

 BEANS AVAILABLE INSTORE

 ALTERNATIVE MILK

 WIFI

CYCLE FRIENDLY

 OUTDOOR seating

FAMILY FRIENDLY

 BRING YOUR OWN Cup

 COFFEE COURSES

www.coffeevolution.co.uk   01484 432881

@coffeevolution   @coffeevolution   @coffeevolutionhuddersfield

ESPRESSO CORNER

11 Kirkgate, Huddersfield, West Yorkshire, HD1 1QS

If you desire a dash of eccentricity with your espresso, this kooky coffee shop in the centre of Huddersfield offers plenty to attract the design-savvy speciality seeker.

Old school desks – complete with graffiti – and a bike mounted on the wall create a striking setting in which to sip Square Mile's fruity Red Brick blend or Dark Woods' Great Taste award winning Under Milk Wood (all caramel loveliness when served with steamed milk).

In addition to good coffee, regulars congregate at this heart-of-the-community cafe to drool over the delicious display of decadent cakes. Head to the counter to eye up the spread of scrumptiousness which ranges from white chocolate and raspberry blondies to homemade crumbly shortbread – with plenty to gratify gluten dodgers.

TIP DON'T MISS THE LEGENDARY HOMEMADE MILLIONAIRE'S SHORTBREAD

A lunch menu of grilled sarnies and salads makes a match for the most gluttonous of appetites. Tuck into a griddled pesto, sundried tomato and halloumi number on thick-cut sourdough bread.

ESTABLISHED
2013

KEY ROASTER
Square Mile
Coffee Roasters

BREWING METHODS
Espresso, V60,
AeroPress

MACHINE
La Marzocco
Linea PB

GRINDER
Mazzer Major E

OPENING HOURS
Mon-Fri
8am-6pm
Sat 9am-5pm
Sun 11am-5pm

 Gluten FREE

 BEANS AVAILABLE INSTORE

 ALTERNATIVE MILK

 WIFI

 DISABLED ACCESS

07595 171846

@espressocorner   @espressocorner

115. BLOC

19a Huddersfield Road, Holmfirth, West Yorkshire, HD9 2JR

Whether you're a member of the smashed avo and egg fraternity, more of a manchego and chorizo fan or a straight up peanut butter purist, you'll find something tasty on toast at this basilica to grilled bread.

Bar the Dark Woods coffee and collection of Canton teas, almost everything at the contemporary cafe is served via the king of carbs. Flavour mash-ups from the creative bunch in the kitchen change regularly depending on the local producers' latest haul and include seasonal specials such as eggy bread with mascarpone, blueberries and toasted almonds.

Bloc's signature splashes of bright yellow span from the alfresco seating to the custom La Marzocco machine, where you'll find an energetic bunch of baristas pulling top-notch espresso based brews with beans from the west Yorkshire roaster.

TIP THE USUAL COMPLIMENTARY BICCY IS SWITCHED FOR A SIDE OF POPCORN

The sunshine vibe has even made its way onto owner Meg Beever's new toy: a converted Land Rover Defender kitted out with a smaller La Marzocco model and K30 grinder. Find it fuelling speciality worshippers at festivals and private events across the county.

ESTABLISHED
2016

KEY ROASTER
Dark Woods
Coffee

BREWING METHOD
Espresso,
V60, batch filter

MACHINE
La Marzocco
Linea Classic

GRINDER
Cimbali Magnum

Mon, Wed-Sat
9am-5pm
Sun 10am-4pm

www.bloctoast.co.uk   01484 687228

@blocholmfirth   @bloc_toast   @bloc_toast

116. THE HEPWORTH CAFE

The Hepworth Wakefield, Gallery Walk, Wakefield, West Yorkshire, WF1 5AW

Photo: Evoke Media Group

When a *MasterChef* finalist joins forces with one of Leeds' best looking coffee shops, you know the result is going to be deliciously photogenic.

Taking over The Hepworth Cafe at Wakefield's award winning museum and art gallery in October 2017, executive chef Chris Hale of Pop Up North Catering and the team behind House of Koko have crafted a beautiful space to eat, drink and absorb a slice of culture.

While art lovers fresh from the latest exhibition throng here for their fill of locally sourced and homemade fodder, it's also popular with hot-deskers and caffeine excursionists thanks to the healthy stock of North Star coffee which includes three different bean options for espresso, batch brew and V60.

TIP THE CAFE TRANSFORMS INTO A BAR, DANCE AND PARTY VENUE AFTER DARK

The Hepworth's popular bill of breakfast, brunch and lunch plates changes by the season and includes plenty of options for plant-based visitors. Tuck into your pick of the Yorkshire-inspired delights in the scenic outside seating area or among the fronds in the much-Instagrammed cafe space.

ESTABLISHED
2017

KEY ROASTER
North Star
Coffee Roasters

BREWING METHOD
Espresso, V60,
batch brew

MACHINE
La Marzocco
Linea PB

GRINDER
Mahlkonig EK43,
Fiorenzato
F64 Evo

OPENING HOURS
Mon-Sun
10am-5pm

 Gluten FREE

 BEANS AVAILABLE INSTORE

 ALTERNATIVE MILK

 WIFI

 CYCLE FRIENDLY

 OUTDOOR seating

 FAMILY FRIENDLY

 DISABLED ACCESS

BRING YOUR OWN Cup

www.thehepworthcafe.co.uk   01924 247371

@thehepworthcafe   @thehepworthcafe   @thehepworthcafe

ROASTERS

NORTH
AND
WEST YORKSHIRE

ARTEMIS™

YORKSHIRE

COLD BREWED
COFFEE CONCENTRATE

BEST CHILLED

MAP: 117. ROOST COFFEE & ROASTERY

6 Talbot Yard, Yorkersgate, Malton, North Yorkshire, YO17 7FT

This Malton marvel is a proper family affair. The roastery is run from a former carriage house by David and Ruth Elkington, with help from pint-sized apprentices Erin, Betsy and Skye the goldendoodle.

It's one of six artisan food and drink units housed in the 18th century outbuildings of the Grade II-listed Talbot Hotel, and part of the Made in Malton initiative.

Since the carriage doors were opened to the public in 2015, visiting coffee buffs have been able to venture in to the purpose-built bar to enjoy an espresso or pourover to the mesmerising whir of the Diedrich roaster.

And with a huge stock of house-roasted single origins and blends to choose from, whatever you can't sip in store you can haul home for round two à la cafetiere.

'MADE IN MALTON CONNECTS ARTISAN PRODUCERS TO SPREAD MALTON'S FOODIE REP'

If you don't know where to start, plump for signature blend ROOST, which offers sweet nut and apricot tasting notes when served as espresso, while filter fans can get a rich choc and stone fruit hit in NEST.

ESTABLISHED
2015

ROASTER
MAKE & SIZE
Diedrich IR-12
12kg

CAFE
ONSITE

OPEN
BY APPOINTMENT

BEANS
AVAILABLE
ONLINE ONSITE

---

www.roostcoffee.co.uk   T: 01653 697635

f @roostcoffeeandroastery   🐦 @roost_coffee   📷 @roost_coffee

MAP 118. YORK COFFEE EMPORIUM

Unit 4-5, Rose Centre, York Business Park, York, North Yorkshire, YO26 6RX

At any given time, York Coffee Emporium holds over 35 different single origin coffees, rotating beans to offer seasonal specialities.

An ensemble of roasters are fired up daily at the York roastery where Q grader Laurence and head roaster Richard orchestrate the careful bronzing of the small batch beans. The team of ten are specialists in bespoke blending, and use various methods and profiles to maximise unique flavour notes in the selection of single origins.

Take a tour to see the method behind the magic and get a peek at the reconditioned vintage Otto Swadlo drum roaster – just remember to book in advance.

'TAKE A TOUR TO SEE THE METHOD BEHIND THE MAGIC'

Throughout summer 2018, York Coffee Emporium rebranded and refreshed its e-commerce website so that, while you can still buy beans at the roastery, its coffee is now even more accessible to everyone regardless of budget, experience or location.

Coffee folk across the country can also sign up for the subscription service, where a fortnightly roaster's choice of coffee is delivered to your door.

ESTABLISHED
2012

ROASTER
MAKE & SIZE
Vintage Probat 25kg
Sivetz 18kg
Otto Swadlo 5kg
Solar 2kg

OPEN
BY APPOINTMENT

COFFEE
COURSES

BEANS
AVAILABLE
ONLINE / ONSITE

---

www.yorkcoffeeemporium.co.uk   T: 01904 799399

f @yorkemporiumcoffee   🐦 @york_emporium   📷 @york_emporium

MAP № 119. CASA ESPRESSO

Unit 5, Briar Rhydding, Otley Road, Shipley, West Yorkshire, BD17 7JW

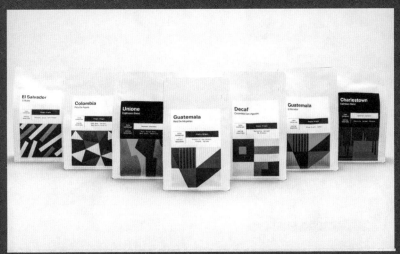

Bradford's first micro roaster flung wide the roastery doors in 2015 to bring its handcrafted riches to the region's speciality enthusiasts.

Nino Di Rienzo and team were hardly newbies on the coffee scene however; for 15 years the close-knit crew had been supporting shops and restaurants across Yorkshire to produce cracking cuppas through training and technical support.

ESTABLISHED
2015

ROASTER
MAKE & SIZE
Probat 5kg

COFFEE COURSES

BEANS AVAILABLE
ONLINE | ONSITE

'THE BRAZILIAN-SUMATRAN CHARLESTOWN ESPRESSO BLEND BAGGED A GOLD AT THE GREAT TASTE AWARDS'

The roots of the business remain and the gang still supply espresso machine equipment and training to wholesale customers. In recent years they've also focused on giving global – and ethically sourced – greens the heat treatment in their own range of bangin' blends.

Casa virgin? First stop on your tasting experience has to be the Brazilian-Sumatran Charlestown Espresso (all rich dark choc and biscuit notes) which bagged a gold at the 2017 Great Taste awards. Pick up a bag, complete with beautiful new branding, from the roastery or website.

---

www.casaespresso.co.uk   T: 01274 595841

f @casaespresso   🐦 @casa_espresso   📷 @casa_espresso

MAP N° 120. NORTH STAR COFFEE ROASTERS

Unit 33, The Boulevard, Leeds Dock, Leeds, West Yorkshire, LS10 1PZ

Alex Kragiopoulos, co-founder and chief roaster at North Star, began his relationship with coffee in Kenya in 2011 when he was conducting research into whether Fairtrade schemes had brought social and economic development to coffee suppliers in Nyeri.

Having met the community, seen the love that went into their work and tasted the wonderful coffee that was produced, he returned home with an ambition to focus on quality speciality producers around the world.

Establishing North Star with co-founder Holly in 2013, the roastery was the first of its kind in Leeds to roast beans of the highest grade and work with speciality-focused arabica farmers.

'THE ROASTERY WAS THE FIRST OF ITS KIND IN LEEDS TO ROAST BEANS OF THE HIGHEST GRADE'

Today, the team strive to roast the best coffee they can get their hands on, sourcing in a way that puts the producer first and ensures their farming is profitable.

The roasts change from season to season as Alex and Holly purchase fresh green coffee in small batches all year round and often feature exclusive micro lots on the menu at the roastery cafe.

ESTABLISHED
2013

ROASTER
MAKE & SIZE
Giesen W15
15kg

CAFE ONSITE

OPEN BY APPOINTMENT

COFFEE COURSES

COURSES

BEANS AVAILABLE
ONLINE   ONSITE

www.northstarroast.com T: 07725 144204

f @northstarcoffeeroasters 🐦 @northstarroast 📷 @northstarroast

№ 121. DARK WOODS COFFEE

Holme Mills, West Slaithwaite Road, Marsden, Huddersfield, West Yorkshire, HD7 6LS

It's been another busy year for the growing team at Dark Woods. The Huddersfield roastery has added ten Great Taste gongs to its sizeable silverware collection and this awards success has secured the privilege of roasting for Liberty London's new food hall.

All of the prize-winning blends, exclusive micro lots and seasonal single origins that make their way to speciality coffee shops across the country are roasted at a renovated textile mill on the banks of the River Colne.

Founders Paul, Ian and Damian bring a wealth of experience, including international competition judging, green coffee buying, high-end coffee consultancy and education to the high spec roastery. Together with SCA-approved trainer Tom, the guys offer serious support for their wholesale customers.

'THE ROASTERY HAS TEAMED UP WITH THE WORLD COFFEE RESEARCH INSTITUTE'

In an ongoing commitment to sustainability, the roastery has also teamed up with the World Coffee Research institute on a groundbreaking project designed to optimise varietal growth and develop new strains of coffee plants better suited to increasingly challenging environmental conditions.

ESTABLISHED
2013

ROASTER
MAKE & SIZE
Vintage Probat
UG22
Probatone 5kg

COFFEE COURSES
 COURSES
 BEANS AVAILABLE

www.darkwoodscoffee.co.uk   T: 01484 843141
f @darkwoodscoffee @darkwoodscoffee @darkwoodscoffee

MAP № 122. GRUMPY MULE

Bewley's, Bent Ley Road, Meltham, Holmfirth, West Yorkshire, HD9 4EP

Grumpy Mule aims to make customers smile with its irreverent, no nonsense and tongue-in-cheek brand. The roastery's unusual name harks back to the days when mules were used to haul coffee cherries down the mountains.

'If that was your nine-to-five job, we reckon you'd have a case of the grumps as well,' says assistant brand manager Scott Lambert.

Nestled in the undulating hills of the Holme Valley, the roastery never seems to sleep. Two gas-fired Probat drum roasters and a Loring Smart roaster are tools for the roastery's trade and have turned out some winning coffee. The company has won 38 Great Taste awards since 2014 – for both its roasted-to-order batch coffee and the retail range. The roastery (which also runs SCA-accredited courses) lives by the following ethos: traceable, ethical, sustainable and arabica.

'THE MULE OFFERS ALL THE GREAT FLAVOURS YOU'D EXPECT WITH SOME SPECIAL TREATS THAT YOU WOULDN'T'

'We hold these standards so our work benefits everyone, whether it's through Fairtrade, direct trade or working with organic farmers and growers,' adds Scott.

ESTABLISHED
2006

ROASTER
MAKE & SIZE
Probat G120 120kg
Probat G60 60kg
Loring Kestrel 35kg

COFFEE COURSES

COURSES

BEANS AVAILABLE

ONLINE

---

www.grumpymule.co.uk   T: 01484 855500

f @grumpymulecoffee   🐦 @grumpymule   📷 @grumpy_mule

123. ARTEMIS COLD BREW COFFEE

Womersley, North Yorkshire, DN6 9BB

You wouldn't compromise on the beans used to craft your morning cappuccino so why settle when it comes to cold caffeine kicks and coffee cocktails?

Now stocked at over 50 indies across the country, Artemis' cold brew has made waves since founder Ben Barker launched the product in 2015.

With an emphasis on sustainability and traceability, Artemis sources the highest quality beans to craft the two-time Great Taste award winning drink. Brewed using a different origin for each product, the bottled range makes for a refreshingly fruity hit straight from the fridge.

ESTABLISHED
2015

COLD BREW +NITRO AVAILABLE

ONLINE

ONSITE

'THE LATEST ADDITION TO THE ARTEMIS PORTFOLIO IS AN INGENIOUS COFFEE CONCENTRATE'

Following its success, the team introduced nitro: a smooth Colombian cold brew infused with nitrogen and dispensed on draught (a bit like Guinness) to lend a velvety mouthfeel and creamy note to the black coffee.

The latest addition to the Artemis portfolio is an ingenious coffee concentrate. The result of freshly roasted Brazilian beans, filtered water and a 21-hour cold brew process, the intense espresso hit is the barista-turned-mixologist's secret weapon.

---

www.artemisbrew.co.uk   **T:** 01977 621691

f @artemisbrew   🐦 @artemisbrew   📷 @artemisbrew

NORTHERN ACADEMY OF COFFEE

MAP № 124.

2 Kings Square, York, North Yorkshire, YO1 8BH

Both filter freshers and pro pourers flock to improve their caffeinated craft from some of the country's leading coffeeprenuers at York's Northern Academy of Coffee.

Along with training and consultancy, co-founder Gordon Howell somehow finds time to run two coffee shops with wife Marie, travel the world giving educational talks, and polish his impressive collection of gongs from a host of international comps.

Business partner Jon Skinner's CV is equally impressive. Known as 'the guy who trains trainers', he's developed SCA, C&G and BSA courses (any other acronyms, anyone?) over 20 years and is considered a true pioneer in pro barista training.

There's no letup at the York training ground; innovation and a focus on current trends mean that training is constantly evolving, so novices, pros and competitors all benefit from bang-up-to-date schooling in the one-to-one sessions.

'INNOVATION AND A FOCUS ON CURRENT TRENDS MEAN THAT TRAINING IS CONSTANTLY EVOLVING'

And after the hard graft of grinding, brewing and pouring, freshly tamped recruits can enjoy a well-earned brew at the on-site cafe.

ESTABLISHED
2013

CAFE
ONSITE

COFFEE
COURSES

COURSES

BEANS
AVAILABLE
ONSITE

www.northernacademyofcoffee.com   07903 123642

@northernacademyofcoffee

MAP 125

NORTH STAR COFFEE ACADEMY

Unit 33, The Boulevard, Leeds Dock, Leeds, West Yorkshire, LS10 1PZ

As if the team at North Star weren't busy enough roasting a line-up of single origin coffees, operating a popular coffee shop and jetting off to origin, the coffee pros also have a training facility in their portfolio.

ESTABLISHED
2016

Running bespoke and accredited courses with the SCA Coffee Skills Program, North Star's speciality timetable includes Barista Skills (teaching the most up-to-date standards and theory), Brewing (a masterclass in brew methods, including what factors to take into account and selecting the right coffee) and Sensory Skills (the sensory analysis of coffee, honing the palate and vocabulary).

The knowledgeable rabble of roasters and trainers also run the North Star Coffee Programme, created specifically to offer training and education in some of the most common problem areas, with courses aimed at those wanting to make the most of their coffee kit at home.

'THE KNOWLEDGEABLE ROASTERS AND TRAINERS ALSO RUN THE NORTH STAR COFFEE PROGRAMME'

The space has been specially designed to be sensory neutral and to provide the optimum environment for learning. It's super accessible too – just a short walk from Leeds station – and even has an on-site hotel.

www.northstarroast.com   07725 144204

@northstarcoffeeroasters   @northstarroast   @northstarroast

SOUTH AND EAST YORKSHIRE & LINCOLNSHIRE

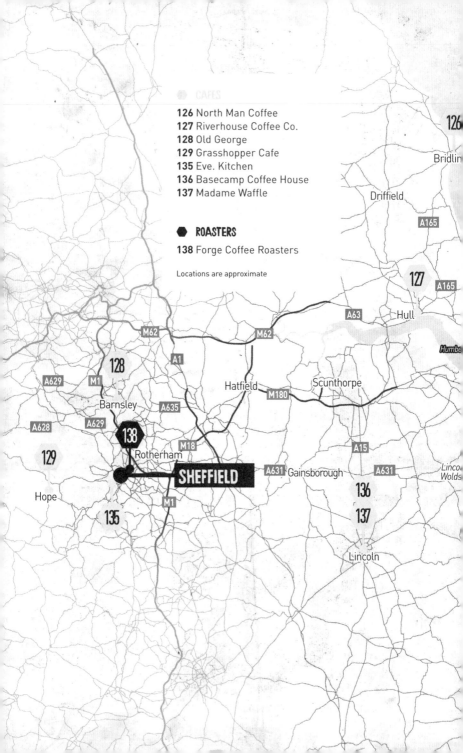

CAFES

126 North Man Coffee
127 Riverhouse Coffee Co.
128 Old George
129 Grasshopper Cafe
135 Eve. Kitchen
136 Basecamp Coffee House
137 Madame Waffle

ROASTERS

138 Forge Coffee Roasters

Locations are approximate

SHEFFIELD

CAFES

130 The Depot Bakery
131 Tamper – Westfield Terrace
132 Marmadukes
133 South Street Kitchen
134 Tamper – Sellers Wheel

Locations are approximate

126. NORTH MAN COFFEE

7 Manor Street, Bridlington, East Yorkshire, YO15 2SA

Flying the flag for veggie (and often organic) food in this seaside town of a thousand fish and chips shops, North Man is a vibrant beacon in a sea of culinary beige.

Every kaleidoscopic creation is made in house – from the fresh bread and the spicy relish slathered on fragrant bean burgers to the fruit-studded vegan scones which festoon the counter.

TIP TRY THE HOMEMADE CASHEW MILK MADE WITH ORGANIC NUTS AND FILTERED WATER

The recent addition of a NutraMilk machine has also enabled the team to create a range of dairy-free milks which are perfect paired with espresso from the likes of Square Mile, Workshop and Casa Espresso.

If you prefer your brew black, plump for an AeroPress or Kalita and sample the latest guest from Somerset's Round Hill Roastery.

Find a spot in the sociable space and in summer sip your flattie alfresco on streetside seating.

ESTABLISHED
2016

KEY ROASTER
Multiple roasters

BREWING METHOD
Espresso, AeroPress, Kalita Wave

MACHINE
La Marzocco FB80

GRINDER
Mythos One Clima Pro, Mahlkonig EK43

OPENING HOURS
Mon-Sat
8am-5pm
Sun 10am-3pm

Gluten FREE

BEANS AVAILABLE INSTORE

ALTERNATIVE MILK

FAMILY FRIENDLY

OUTDOOR seating

01262 673530

@northmancoffee   @northmancoffee

RIVERHOUSE COFFEE CO.

147a Ground Floor, High Street, Hull, East Yorkshire, HU1 1LA

If the Outkast lyrics scribbled on the window of this Old Town newbie don't turn your head, the waft of freshly pulled espresso has the power to persuade passersby to lend their new neighbour some sugar.

Joining Hull's burgeoning coffee scene in 2017, the team wasted no time in cementing their speciality status. They got together with fellow Hullensians, The Blending Room, to knock up a knockout roast for their contemporary coffee shop.

Depending on the time of year – and whether the sun is shining in east Yorkshire – you can sample the seasonally changing beans as steaming espresso and batch filter, or chilled homemade cold brew and coffee lemonade (cold brew, espresso, lemon syrup and tonic).

TIP BUY A LOAF AND ANOTHER WILL BE DONATED TO SOMEONE IN NEED IN THE COMMUNITY

During the week, rumbling tums are sated with a selection of breakfast bites and stacked sarnies which have been crafted at the sister bakery. However, we reckon greedy trips to Riverhouse are best reserved for the weekend when the brunch game gets serious: slow poached duck eggs with ham hock and hollandaise goes down great with a flat white.

ESTABLISHED
2017

KEY ROASTER
The Blending Room

BREWING METHOD
Espresso, batch filter, cold brew

MACHINE
Sanremo Verona RS

GRINDER
Nuova Simonelli Mythos One

OPENING HOURS
Mon-Fri
8.45am-5pm
Sat 9am-5pm
Sun 10am-4pm

Gluten FREE

BEANS AVAILABLE
INSTORE

ALTERNATIVE MILK

WIFI

OUTDOOR seating

BRING YOUR OWN cup

www.riverhousecoffeeco.co.uk   01482 210253

@riverhousecoffeeco   @rhcoffeeco   @riverhousecoffeeco

128. OLD GEORGE

14 Market Hill, Barnsley, South Yorkshire, S70 2QE

Barnsley's brew buffs have been supremely happy – and well caffeinated – since Old George rocked up in 2017.

Owner Gareth Derbyshire puts it down to his unique bill of homemade fare and Yorkshire-roasted coffee, saying: 'No one else around here offers the coffee and menu that we have.'

To remain at the top of their game, the crew are constantly cooking up new ways to satisfy their coffee community. Since opening, Gareth has upped the cafe's caffeine offering with new brew methods, employed a three-strong band of baristas to craft the Forge beans, developed the 'blue room' upstairs for those who like a view with their brew, and opened up the space for parties and events.

TIP SWEET TOOTH? TRY THE GEORGE BROWNIE – IT WOULD BE RUDE NOT TO

On the food front, things are also moving in a satisfyingly fresh direction. A new menu offers up comforting fodder to accompany the coffee: don't miss the warm sweet-cured bacon and cheddar focaccia for an oozing boost to your day.

ESTABLISHED
2017

KEY ROASTER
Forge Coffee Roasters

BREWING METHOD
Espresso, V60, batch brew, AeroPress

MACHINE
La Marzocco Strada EP

GRINDER
Anfim

OPENING HOURS
Thu-Fri
9am-7pm
Sat-Wed
9am-5pm

www.old-george.co.uk | 01226 217169
@oldgeorgebarn @oldgeorgebarn @oldgeorgebarnsley

MAP 129.

129. GRASSHOPPER CAFE

18 Castleton Road, Hope, Derbyshire, S33 6RD

Photo: Dan Cook

Just 25 minutes outside Sheffield and in the heart of the Peaks, Grasshopper is the go-to for a pre-cycle speciality hit, and where walkers aim to finish any ramble.

You don't have to be a yomper, fell runner or road cyclist to find a warm welcome at this beautiful little cafe, however. Owners Graham and Mel have cultivated just as loyal an audience in the retired villagers who pop by for their daily shot.

TIP PUT IN THE MILES FOR A FULL ENGLISH BREKKIE SERVED ON DERBYSHIRE OATCAKE

Stonking cheese toasties, Smith Street coffee, creative salads, homemade slices, Cooper the garden cat and even, occasionally, wood-fired pizza in the garden are all spokes in Grasshopper's wheel of fame.

Graham cranks out top-notch brews on the Sanremo Capri, featuring regular guests such as North Star and Heart and Graft.

On the weekend you may have to battle it out with a bloke in Lycra for a seat, but swing by on a weekday and you can steal a spot by the wood burner – or out in the lavender in summer.

ESTABLISHED
2016

KEY ROASTER
Multiple roasters

BREWING METHOD
Espresso

MACHINE
Sanremo Capri

GRINDER
Mazzer Major

OPENING HOURS
Thu-Tue
9.30am-4pm

 Gluten FREE

 BEANS AVAILABLE / INSTORE

 ALTERNATIVE MILK

 WIFI

CYCLE FRIENDLY

OUTDOOR SEATING

FAMILY FRIENDLY

 DISABLED ACCESS

07976 067338

@hoppercafehope   @hoppercafe   @hoppercafe

130. THE DEPOT BAKERY

92 Burton Road, Kelham Island, Sheffield, South Yorkshire, S3 8DA

Two of life's pleasures are honoured at Depot: great bread and coffee. So it's no surprise that this funky bakery cafe in Kelham Island is always jam packed.

Everything's made out back – from the sourdough rolls stuffed with ham hock, wensleydale and celeriac to the salty-sweet peanut butter slice with its slick of chocolate ganache.

The space is light, airy and the epitome of urban regeneration, and as popular with laptop lingerers and long lunchers as those swooping in for a coffee and loaf to-go.

TIP THE SOURDOUGH CULTURES ARE NAMED DAVE, RYAN AND WALTER

Plump for the house blend by Ozone, do Dark Woods on filter or, if you've reached peak caffeine, try a West Coast Cocoa Mayan Chilli Hot Chocolate.

Owner Jon's Kiwi heritage shines through in the emphasis on quality food and drink, along with friendly, nothing-is-too-much-trouble service. And while everything is sourced locally or made in house, he's rooting for his home team with the range of organic and Fairtrade NZ sodas.

ESTABLISHED
2014

KEY ROASTER
Multiple roasters

BREWING METHOD
Espresso, batch brew

MACHINE
La Marzocco Linea

GRINDER
Mythos One Clima Pro

OPENING HOURS
Mon-Sun
9am-4pm

www.thedepotbakery.co.uk   01142 757779

@thedepotbakery   @thedepotbakery   @thedepotbakery

TAMPER – WESTFIELD TERRACE

9 Westfield Terrace, Sheffield, South Yorkshire, S1 4GH

WESTFIELD TERRACE

This is a coffee lover's coffee joint. Focused more on the ol' black magic than cafe food (although there is a new menu), most caffeine fiends swing by for a cortado at the counter or a shot-on-the-trot.

Diminutive, moody and sporting a fresh outfit of polished concrete, Tamper is 100 per cent speciality cool. It's also well positioned at the edge of indie-tastic Division Street for a caffeinated livener on your vintage shopping trawl.

MONTHLY TASTING SESSIONS ARE A CHANCE TO POLISH YOUR COFFEE KNOWLEDGE

The enthusiastic baristas are always up for sharing their delight in the Ozone house blend and the latest guest roasts, so there's plenty of good quality coffee chat to pair with your pick of the beans.

Not up to being sociable before you've had your morning flattie? Fear not, there's plenty of coffee reading matter to hide behind too.

Treat yourself to a toastie made from stonking sourdough which is handcrafted at sister bakery The Depot at Kelham Island.

ESTABLISHED
2011

KEY ROASTER
Multiple roasters

BREWING METHODS
Espresso,
Kalita Wave,
Chemex,
AeroPress

MACHINE
La Marzocco
Strada EP

GRINDER
Mahlkonig EK43,
Mythos One
Clima Pro

OPENING HOURS
Mon-Fri
8am-4.30pm
Sat 9am-4pm
Sun 10am-4pm

www.tampercoffee.co.uk   01143 271080

@tampercoffee   @tampercoffee   @tampercoffeewt

MAP 132.

MARMADUKES

22 Norfolk Row, Sheffield, South Yorkshire, S1 2PA

In a city that can rightly crow about its plethora of indies, this coffee shop stands out from the flock – especially if you're up for European-style coffee sipping and people watching while perched at an alfresco table.

The rustic-meets-Mediterranean vibe, homemade food and quirky decor are very attractive, but don't go thinking that coffee is the also-ran here.

Claire, TJ and the family team are as exacting about extraction as any hip coffee bar and supplement the house single origin beans with a pleasing merry-go-round of serve styles and guests from the likes of Somerset's Round Hill and Berlin's The Barn.

TIP BRUNCH BECOMES AN ALL-DAY AFFAIR ON SUNDAYS

A new range of cold drinks, including a citrus iced tea brewed in house, has been introduced this year, along with the launch of Marmadukes' online shop which sells the same homemade cakes you can scoff in store. As yet, you can't order an accompanying piccolo for delivery – though a new site in the pipeline for later this year promises a second helping of the Marmadukes experience.

ESTABLISHED
2012

KEY ROASTER
Origin Coffee Roasters

BREWING METHOD
Espresso, batch brew, Chemex, Kalita Wave

MACHINE
La Marzocco Linea PB

GRINDER
Mythos One Clima Pro, Mazzer Robur, Mahlkonig EK43

OPENING HOURS
Mon-Sat
9am-5pm
Sun 10am-4pm

www.marmadukes.co 01142 767462

@marmadukescafe @marmadukescafe @marmadukescafe

MAP 1.3.3. # SOUTH STREET KITCHEN

19-20 South Street, Park Hill, Sheffield, South Yorkshire, S2 5QX

The first thing you need to know about this place is that it's not easy to find; the second is that it's absolutely worth making the effort.

On the ground level of the legendary (and now Urban Splash-regenerated) Park Hill flats, South Street Kitchen revels in a Scandi-meets-concrete-cool-by-way-of-the-Middle-East vibe. This isn't freshly poured and polished concrete of the hipster variety though. This is the original fabric of an architectural gem that's been stripped back to its skeleton in a total next-gen reinvention.

TIP THE CAFE IS NEXT TO THE FAMOUS 'I LOVE YOU, WILL YOU MARRY ME?' BRIDGE

On the coffee front, Dark Woods is served with care and accompanied by grub that's fresh, creative and incredible value. Try scrambled tofu for brekkie and the daily changing lunches, then return on a Friday night when the kitchen opens late for its weekly feast.

Salivating for a taste of the action? The easiest way to get here is on foot from the city – it's close to Ponds Forge and the centre, as well as the train station. If you're travelling by car, check the website first for directions as your satnav probably won't find it.

ESTABLISHED
2018

KEY ROASTER
Multiple roasters

BREWING METHOD
Espresso, V60, AeroPress

MACHINE
La Marzocco Linea PB AV

GRINDER
Mahlkonig EK43, Mahlkonig Peak

OPENING HOURS
Tue-Thu 9am-5pm
Fri 9am-10pm
Sat 10am-5pm

www.southstreetkitchen.org   07763 678858

@southstreetkitchen   @southstktchn   @southstreetkitchen

MAP 134. TAMPER – SELLERS WHEEL

149 Arundel Street, Sheffield, South Yorkshire, S1 2NU

Switching things up on a regular basis has been one of the ways Tamper has stayed ahead of the game since Kiwi Jon Perry launched his coffee concept in 2011.

The portfolio is now three-strong, and new at the Sellers Wheel outpost are a cool polished concrete bar, a refresh of the jungle wall mural and the introduction of Dark Woods coffee – as well as a fresh menu.

TAMPER'S NEAR THE TRAIN STATION, SO THIS IS THE FIRST STOP ON ANY SHEFFIELD COFFEE TOUR

'We're trying to push all the time,' says Jon, 'and we aim to be the full package.

'Everything is made to order. The bread (and soon charcuterie) comes from our bakery The Depot, our food is really high quality, the coffee's great and we make sure people have a good time.

'I've just tried to bring the normal standards of a good New Zealand cafe to Sheffield.' Happily, people love it.

It's a lively environment in which to hang out – all plants, wood and industrial red brick – and a taste of paradise (the coffee, food and tropical decor) in the gritty city.

ESTABLISHED
2013

KEY ROASTER
Multiple roasters

BREWING METHODS
Espresso, Kalita Wave, batch brew, AeroPress, cold brew

MACHINE
La Marzocco Linea PB

GRINDER
Mahlkonig Pulse, Mahlkonig EK43

OPENING HOURS
Mon-Thu 8am-5pm
Fri 8am-10pm
Sat 9am-6pm
Sun 9am-4pm

Gluten FREE
BEANS AVAILABLE INSTORE
ALTERNATIVE MILK
WIFI
CYCLE FRIENDLY
OUTDOOR SEATING
FAMILY FRIENDLY
DISABLED ACCESS
BRING YOUR OWN CUP
COFFEE COURSES

www.tampercoffee.co.uk | 01142 757970

f @tampercoffee @tampercoffee @tampercoffeesw

EVE. KITCHEN

380 Sharrow Vale Road, Sheffield, South Yorkshire, S11 8ZP

For those days when you need to be kind to yourself and salad just won't cut it, Eve. Kitchen specialises in the kind of forbidden fruit that's worth a fall off the healthy eating wagon.

Yielding, pillowy doughnuts stuffed with chewy homemade hazelnut ice cream, and sugar-powdered puffs plump with fresh raspberry cream and studded with jewel-like fruit ... yep, that's the kind of temptation we're talking about.

TRY THE SAVOURY DOUGHNUTS SUCH AS OX CHEEK, PAPRIKA SUGAR AND BLACKBERRY JUS

Doughnuts and coffee are the name of the game at Eve. Kitchen – and sin doesn't come into it.

Owner Lauren Eve Hutchinson pulls Dark Woods' Colombian beans and Origin Coffee blends through the machine, then further soothes customers' souls with the likes of doughnut-loaf french toast, lightly fried in butter and served with bacon and maple syrup.

Everything is beautiful, natural and seasonal. It's like the Garden of Eden, but with more alluring inducements.

ESTABLISHED
2015

KEY ROASTER
Dark Woods
Coffee

BREWING METHODS
Espresso,
V60, Chemex

MACHINE
Londinium L2

GRINDER
Compak

OPENING HOURS
Tue-Sat
10am-4pm
Sun 9am-3pm

www.evekitchen.co.uk 07738 280638

@eve_kitchen @eve.kitchen

MAP 136.

136. BASECAMP COFFEE HOUSE

12 Steep Hill, Lincoln, Lincolnshire, LN2 1LT

Tackle the 40 metre climb of the aptly named Steep Hill and you'll enjoy sweet rewards at Basecamp's 13th century building turned coffee house.

The beans enticing intrepid caffeine fans to make such expeditions are bronzed at sister roastery Makushi – one of a small crop of roasteries in this neck of the woods – which focuses solely on single origin and ethically sourced greens.

Try the latest lot as both espresso and V60 (there's also Chemex and AeroPress if you ask) and compare tasting notes. Alternatively, go rogue with an option from the guest coffee list which includes European favourites such as La Cabra, Square Mile, Five Elephant and Outpost.

TIP · TAKE YOUR COFFEE ALFRESCO IN THE UPCYCLED ROOF GARDEN

Motivated to do their bit for the planet, the Basecamp team encourage reducing and reusing, and have swapped disposables for fully biodegrable and compostable cups. The foodie menu is also pretty green: discover lots of veggie, vegan and gluten-free goodies as well as homemade bagels and fresh sourdough bread.

ESTABLISHED
2016

KEY ROASTER
Makushi Coffee Roasters

BREWING METHOD
Espresso, Kalita Wave, V60, Chemex, AeroPress, batch brew

MACHINE
La Marzocco Linea PB

GRINDER
Mythos One Clima Pro, Mahlkonig EK43

OPENING HOURS
Tue-Sun
10am-4pm

 Gluten FREE

 BEANS AVAILABLE INSTORE

 ALTERNATIVE MILK

 WIFI

 CYCLE FRIENDLY

 OUTDOOR seating

 FAMILY Friendly

 BRING YOUR OWN cup.

07472 373991

f @basecamplincoln   @basecamplincoln

137. MADAME WAFFLE

285 High Street, Lincoln, Lincolnshire, LN2 1AL

Whether it's the waft of freshly pressed waffles or the heady scent of espresso that initially lures you in, few leave Madame Waffle without sampling both of her famed indulgences.

Matching caffeine and carbs at their three-storey cafe since 2015, Bruce and Sharon Whetton have created a space where speciality saints and sweet-toothed sinners can gather together to get their fix.

Bruce's obsession with the dark stuff inspired him to bring a slice of the London coffee scene to Lincoln. He's eager to share his passion with the local folk – he's an Authorised Speciality Coffee Trainer as well as the house barista – and showcases Square Mile beans alongside far-flung guests from Germany and Denmark.

TRY THE SO-WRONG-IT'S-RIGHT 'ELVIS': BACON, PEANUT BUTTER, BANANA AND MAPLE SYRUP

Sharon takes charge of the kitchen, fashioning sweet and savoury waffle combos such as halloumi and avocado, chocolate and mandarin, and bacon and banana.

A new building extension is also on the horizon, providing even more room for those perfect pairings.

ESTABLISHED
2015

KEY ROASTER
Square Mile Coffee Roasters

BREWING METHOD
Espresso, V60, AeroPress,

MACHINE
La Marzocco Linea PB

GRINDER
Mythos One x 2, Mahlkonig EK43

OPENING HOURS
Mon-Thu
9am-5pm
Fri-Sat 9am-6pm
Sun 10am-5pm

 Gluten FREE

 BEANS AVAILABLE INSTORE

 ALTERNATIVE MILK

 WIFI

 OUTDOOR seating

 FAMILY friendly

 BRING YOUR OWN cup

 COFFEE COURSES

www.madamewaffle.co.uk 01522 512286

@madamewaffleuk   @madamewaffleuk   @madamewaffle

ROASTERS

SOUTH AND EAST YORKSHIRE & LINCOLNSHIRE

MAP: 138. FORGE COFFEE ROASTERS

Don Road, Sheffield, South Yorkshire, S9 2TF

It's not an easy gig upholding the long-held reputation of Sheffield's master craftsmen, but the coffee roasting crew at Forge are doing a pretty good job of it.

Based in Sheffield's engineering heartland, where the Forge Inn public house once stood, the team have imbued their environment with forging memorabilia from the city's industrial past. *'The Forge oozes traditional charm and character; it fires up our passion for quality craftsmanship,'* say owner Michael and roaster Jack.

ESTABLISHED
2015

ROASTER
MAKE & SIZE
Giesen W30A
30kg

'IT FIRES UP OUR PASSION FOR QUALITY CRAFTSMANSHIP'

Their rather magnificent Giesen W30A undoubtedly provides further inspiration for the team's daily handcrafting of their beany bounty.

Current must-try blends include the crowd-pleasing dark choc and black cherry-ish Invicta, and the honey and orange-spiked Ruskin.

The gang still manage to fit in on-the-road hijinks around their busy schedule, regularly taking their 1935 Bedford truck (Bar 124) and 1933 Austin 7 out to events.

www.forgecoffeeroasters.co.uk   T: 01142 441361

f @forgeroasters   🐦 @forgeroasters   📷 @forgeroasters

SO MANY EXCEPTIONAL PLACES TO DRINK COFFEE

1901 CAFFE BISTRO
68 St George's Terrace, Jesmond,
Newcastle upon Tyne, NE2 2DL

ANCOATS COFFEE CO.
9 Royal Mills, 17 Redhill Street,
Manchester, M4 5BA
www.ancoats-coffee.co.uk

ANOTHER HEART TO FEED
West Village, 220 Burton Road, West Didsbury,
Greater Manchester, M20 2LW
www.anotherhearttofeed.com

ARCH SIXTEEN CAFE
Arch 16, High Level Parade, Wellington Street,
Gateshead, Tyne and Wear, NE8 2AJ
www.archsixteen.com

BLANCHFLOWER
12-14 Shaw's Road, Altrincham,
Greater Manchester, WA14 1QU
www.blanchflower.co

BLK COFFEE
214 Chillingham Road, Heaton,
Newcastle upon Tyne, NE6 5LP
www.blkcoffee.co.uk

BLOOMING SKULL COFFEE
138 Bebington Road, Bebington, Wirral,
Merseyside, CH62 5BJ
www.bloomingskullcoffee.co.uk

BRAGAZZIS
224-226 Abbeydale Road, Sheffield,
South Yorkshire, S7 1FL
www.bragazzis.co.uk

CAFÉ 164
Munro House, Duke Street, Leeds,
West Yorkshire, LS9 8AG
www.cafe164.com

CAFFEINATED
Trinity Indoor Market, Market Lane, Hull,
East Yorkshire, HU1 2JH

CIELO COFFEE – EXPRESS

Garforth Library, 1-5 Main Street, Garforth,
Leeds, West Yorkshire, LS25 1DU

www.cielouk.com

CIELO COFFEE – GARFORTH

41 Main Street, Garforth, Leeds,
West Yorkshire, LS25 1DS

www.cielouk.com

CIELO COFFEE – YORK PLACE

18 York Place, Leeds,
West Yorkshire, LS1 2EX

www.cielouk.com

COFFEE & FANDISHA

5 Brick Street, Liverpool, Merseyside, L1 0BL

COFFEE AROMA

24 Guildhall Street, Lincoln,
Lincolnshire, LN1 1TR

www.coffeearoma.co.uk

COFFEE FIX

80 Church Road, Gatley, Cheadle,
Greater Manchester, SK8 4NQ

www.wearecoffeefix.com

EMILY'S BY DE LUCA BOUTIQUE

72-74 Market Street, Thornton, Bradford,
West Yorkshire, BD13 3HF

www.delucaboutique.co.uk

EXCHANGE COFFEE COMPANY – BLACKBURN MARKET

Stall F9, Blackburn Market,
Ainsworth Street, Blackburn,
Lancashire, BB1 5AF

www.exchangecoffee.co.uk

EXCHANGE COFFEE COMPANY – TODMORDEN

Market Hall, Burnley Road, Todmorden,
West Yorkshire, OL14 5AJ

www.exchangecoffee.co.uk

FILTER + FOX

27 Duke Street, Liverpool,
Merseyside, L1 5AP

www.filterandfox.co.uk

FLAT WHITE KITCHEN

40 Saddler Street, Durham,
Tyne and Wear, DH1 3NU

www.flatwhitekitchen.com

FORGE BAKEHOUSE

302 Abbeydale Road, Sheffield,
South Yorkshire, S7 1FL

www.forgebakehouse.co.uk

GOURMET COFFEE BAR

29 Bridge Road, Wrexham,
North Wales, LL13 9QS

www.gourmetcoffeebar.co.uk

GREENSMITH & THACKWRAY

30 St Nicholas Street, Scarborough,
North Yorkshire, YO11 2HF

www.greensmiththackwray.com

GRINDSMITH – THE POD

Greengate Square, Victoria Bridge Street,
Manchester, M3 5AS

www.grindsmith.com

THE GRUB & GROG SHOP

3 Sheaf Street, Leeds,
West Yorkshire, LS10 1HD

www.grubandgrog.co.uk

HATCH COFFEE

Former parking attendants cabin,
Ellison Place, Newcastle upon Tyne, NE1 8XS

www.hatchcoffee.com

IDLE HANDS

35 Dale Street, Northern Quarter,
Manchester, M1 2HF

www.idlehandscoffee.com

IF- COFFEE BAR

43 Call Lane, Leeds, West Yorkshire, LS1 7BT

www.if-coffeebar.co.uk

JOE'SPRESSO

404 South Road, Walkley, Sheffield,
South Yorkshire, S6 3TF

www.joespresso.co.uk

KAPOW COFFEE – THORNTON'S ARCADE

15 Thornton's Arcade, Leeds,
West Yorkshire, LS1 6LQ

LANEWAY & CO

17-19 High Bridge,
Newcastle upon Tyne, NE1 1EW

LOAFERS

Rustic Level, Piece Hall, Halifax,
West Yorkshire, HX1 1RE

www.loafersvinyl.co.uk

LONGFORD CAFE

Longford Park, Manchester, M32 8DA

www.longford.cafe

MANCOCO

Arch 84, Hewitt Street, Manchester, M15 4GB

www.mancoco.co.uk

MARKET HOUSE COFFEE

Altrincham Market House, 26 Market Street,
Altrincham, Greater Manchester, WA14 1SA

www.altrinchammarket.co.uk

MOSS COFFEE

65 Brook Street, Chester, Cheshire, CH1 3DZ

www.mosscoffee.co.uk

MOTHER ESPRESSO
The Tea Factory, 82 Wood Street,
Liverpool, Merseyside, L1 4DQ
www.motherespresso.co.uk

MRS ATHA'S
18 Central Road, Leeds,
West Yorkshire, LS1 6DE
www.mrsathasleeds.com

NORTH TEA POWER
G22, 36 Tib Street, Northern Quarter,
Manchester, M4 1LA
www.northteapower.co.uk

NUMBER 44
44 Sea View Road, Colwyn Bay,
North Wales, LL29 8DG
www.number44.wales

OFF THE GROUND COFFEE HOUSE
63 Grange Road, Middlesbrough,
North Yorkshire, TS1 5AS
www.offthegroundcoffee.co.uk

ONE PERCENT FOREST
42 Allerton Road, Woolton, Liverpool,
Merseyside, L25 7RG
www.onepercentforest.co.uk

OPPOSITE CAFE – BLENHEIM TERRACE
26 Blenheim Terrace, Leeds,
West Yorkshire, LS2 9HD
www.oppositecafe.co.uk

OPPOSITE CAFE – CHAPEL ALLERTON
4 Stainbeck Lane, Chapel Allerton,
Leeds, West Yorkshire, LS7 3QY
www.oppositecafe.co.uk

PANNA KITCHEN & CANTEEN
Silk House Court, Tithebarn Street,
Liverpool, Merseyside, L2 2LZ
www.pannaliverpool.com

PINK LANE COFFEE
1 Pink Lane, Newcastle upon Tyne, NE1 5DW
www.pinklanecoffee.co.uk

POPUP BIKES
Arch 5, Corporation Street,
Manchester, M4 4DG
www.popupbikes.co.uk

PUMP N GRIND
52a Brudenell Road, Leeds,
West Yorkshire, LS6 1BD
www.pumpngrind.co.uk

ROAST COFFEE & KITCHEN
33 Crosby Road North, Waterloo,
Liverpool, Merseyside, L22 4QB
www.roastcoffeeandkitchen.com

SOCIABLE FOLK
10 Wellington Place, Leeds,
West Yorkshire, LS1 4AP
www.sociablefolk.co.uk

STEAM YARD
Unit 1-2 Aberdeen Court,
97 Division Street, Sheffield,
South Yorkshire, S1 4GE
www.steamyard.co.uk

TEA HIVE
53 Manchester Road, Chorlton,
Manchester, M21 9PW
www.teahive.co.uk

TEACUP KITCHEN
53-55 Thomas Street, Manchester, M4 1NA
www.teacupandcakes.com

MORE? THE ARTISAN BAKERY
Middle of Mill Yard, Staveley,
Cumbria, LA8 9LR
www.moreartisan.co.uk

THE BARN @ SCORTON
The Square, Scorton, Preston,
Lancashire, PR3 1AU
www.plantsandgifts.co.uk

THE COMMUTE COFFEE HOUSE
20 Leeds Road, Ilkley,
West Yorkshire, LS29 8DS
www.thecommuteyorkshire.com

THE HANDMADE BAKERY
Unit 6, Upper Mills Canal Side,
Slaithwaite, Huddersfield,
West Yorkshire, HD7 5HA
www.thehandmadebakery.coop

THE PARLOUR
19-21 Wellgate, Clitheroe,
Lancashire, BB7 2DP

THIEVING HARRY'S
73 Humber Street, Hull,
East Yorkshire, HU1 1TU
www.thievingharrys.co.uk

TOP DOOR ESPRESSO
Indoor Shop 45, Halifax Borough Market,
Halifax, West Yorkshire, HX1 1DZ
www.topdoorespresso.uk

TWO GINGERS
Unit 5, Paragon Arcade, Hull,
East Yorkshire, HU1 3PQ
www.twogingerscoffee.co.uk

UPSHOT – GIBRALTAR STREET
169 Gibraltar Street, Sheffield,
South Yorkshire, S3 8UA
www.upshotespresso.co.uk

UPSHOT – GLOSSOP ROAD
355 Glossop Road, Sheffield,
South Yorkshire, S10 2HP
www.upshotespresso.co.uk

WOODLAWN COFFEE CO
60a Town Street, Horsforth, Leeds,
West Yorkshire, LS18 4AP

MORE GOOD ROASTERS

ADDITIONAL PICKS FOR YOUR HOME HOPPER

204
ANCOATS COFFEE CO.
9 Royal Mills, 17 Redhill Street,
Manchester, M4 5BA

www.ancoats-coffee.co.uk

205
BEAN BROTHERS COFFEE COMPANY
Fairfield Mills, Colne Road, Huddersfield,
West Yorkshire, HD1 3DX

www.beanbrothers.co.uk

206
BEAN MILES
Wetheral, Carlisle, Cumbria, CA4 8LD

www.beanmiles.co.uk

207
JOLLY BEAN ROASTERY
15 Victoria Road, Saltaire,
West Yorkshire, BD18 3LQ

www.jollybeanroastery.co.uk

208
LUCKIE BEANS
3 Love Lane, Berwick-upon-Tweed,
Northumberland, TD15 1AR

www.luckiebeans.co.uk

209
MANCOCO
Arch 84, Hewitt Street, Manchester, M15 4GB

www.mancoco.co.uk

210
MAUDE COFFEE ROASTERS
82-83 Railway Street, Leeds,
West Yorkshire, LS9 8HB

www.maudecoffee.co.uk

211
NORTHERN EDGE COFFEE
Unit 5, Meantime Workshops,
Berwick-upon-Tweed,
Northumberland, TD15 1RG

www.northernedgecoffee.co.uk

212
PILGRIMS COFFEE
Falkland House, Marygate, Holy Island,
Northumberland, TD15 2SJ

www.pilgrimscoffee.com

213
PINK LANE COFFEE
19 Back Goldspink Lane,
Newcastle upon Tyne, NE2 1NU

www.pinklanecoffee.co.uk

214
PUMP N GRIND COFFEE ROASTERS
52a Brudenell Road, Leeds,
West Yorkshire, LS6 1BD

www.pumpngrind.co.uk

215
PUMPHREYS COFFEE
Bridge Street, Blaydon,
Newcastle upon Tyne, NE21 4JH

www.pumphreys-coffee.co.uk

216
ROUNTON COFFEE ROASTERS
East Rounton, Northallerton,
North Yorkshire, DL6 2LG

www.rountoncoffee.co.uk

217
SMITH STREET COFFEE ROASTERS
156 Arundel Street, Sheffield,
South Yorkshire, S1 4RE

www.smithstreetcoffeeroasters.co.uk

218
TANK COFFEE
Unit 1, Acorn Business Centre, Leigh,
Greater Manchester, WN7 3DD

www.tankcoffee.com

219
THE BLENDING ROOM
Unit 22 Factory Estate, Boulevard, Hull,
East Yorkshire, HU3 4AY

www.theblendingroom.co.uk

MEET THE COMMITTEE

Our *Independent Coffee Guide* committee is made up of a small band of leading coffee experts from across the region who have worked with Salt Media and the North's coffee community to oversee the creation of this year's guide

DAVE OLEJNIK

HANNAH DAVIES

Having always sought out great coffee shops, it was during Dave's time living in Seattle (where he worked as a touring guitar tech) that he was inspired to divert his energy into coffee. Returning to the UK, he worked for Coffee Community and travelled the world as a trainer and consultant before launching Laynes Espresso in Leeds in 2011.

Knocking through into a neighbouring building at the start of 2017, he's increased the popular cafe's capacity from 15 to 55 covers.

Hannah's 12-year career in the coffee industry saw her develop from a barista in Liverpool to training manager and authorised SCA (Specialty Coffee Association) trainer for a national coffee company. Her current role as SCA events manager allows her to fulfil her commitment to the coffee community in the UK and across Europe.

Since 2014, Hannah has worked with the Manchester coffee scene to create Manchester Coffee Festival, dedicated to showcasing the speciality coffee industry in the North.

PAUL MEIKLE-JANNEY

IAN STEEL

Paul is one of the founders of Dark Woods Coffee, a multi-award winning roastery based in a renovated textile mill in the Pennine Hills on the outskirts of Huddersfield.

Paul's connection to coffee goes back to 1999 when he started Coffee Community, an international training and consultancy agency for the speciality industry. Within his role he has co-written both the City & Guilds and SCA barista qualifications.

Involved in the World and UK Barista Championships from their inception, he was a head judge for the World Latte Art and World Coffee in Good Spirits championships for four years.

Nowadays, when he's not fulfilling SCA Education Committee duties, Paul tends to his ever-growing jazz and house record collection.

Ian has enjoyed two careers: one as a TV producer and the other as a coffee roaster. '*They're both related,*' he says, '*as they involve seeing ideas through from conception to completion.*' A vital part of his current role as keeper of the flame at Atkinsons is storytelling – his online journal was recently listed in the Best 40 Coffee Blogs in the World.

Standing in the middle of the coffee chain between producer and consumer, Ian sees his responsibility to help make connections between the two. His goal is for all Atkinsons beans to be 'relationship coffees', working with the farmers to create financial and environmental sustainability and full traceability.

Ian is also an entrepreneur-in-residence and honorary teaching fellow at Lancaster University's Management School and a founding member of the Global Eco-Innovation forum.

COFFEE NOTES

Somewhere to save details of specific brews and
beans you've enjoyed

COFFEE
NOTES

Somewhere to save details of specific brews and
beans you've enjoyed

COFFEE NOTES

Somewhere to save details of specific brews and beans you've enjoyed

INDEX

INDEX

THE NORTH
AND NORTH WALES
INDEPENDENT
COFFEE
GUIDE

the INSIDER'S GUIDE TO SPECIALITY
COFFEE VENUES AND ROASTERS

★★★★★★★★★★★

№ 4